Benjamin Bartis Comegys

An Order of Worship

With forms of prayer for divine service

Benjamin Bartis Comegys

An Order of Worship
With forms of prayer for divine service

ISBN/EAN: 9783337037697

Printed in Europe, USA, Canada, Australia, Japan

Cover: Foto ©Lupo / pixelio.de

More available books at **www.hansebooks.com**

PREFACE.

THIS BOOK is a compilation; its materials being drawn from service books in use in the Church of Scotland, the Church of England, the Huguenot Church of Charleston, S. C., and from other sources.

Some such thoughts as these have seemed to make it worth while to prepare it.

I wish to submit some models of public prayer which are direct, simple, scriptural and devotional. Many spoken prayers are indirect, obscure, unscriptural and undevotional. It does not at all follow that such so-called prayers create or suggest true devotion in those who are expected to join in them, because the speaker is warmed into a glow of intellectual fervor in making them.

In places where there are no churches, and where, except perhaps in a Sunday-School, there are no public religious services, a Superintendent of a Sunday-School, or any other person, can, with these forms, maintain public services without the necessity for extempore prayers, from which many good people shrink or refrain. There is, however, a place for special or extempore prayers in every service. A young preacher, who has spent more time in learning how to make sermons than in learning how to offer prayers in appropriate language, may be aided in his pulpit ministrations by the use of these prayers, to which he may add others of his own composing, written and read, or spoken from memory or extempore.

" It cannot but appear strange that, while sermons are composed with so much care and pains, we should leave our prayers altogether to the impulse of the moment; as if it were more needful that our speeches to our fellow-men should be well ordered than our addresses to God. In every point of view, extempore preaching is far more natural and becoming than extempore prayer, because any want of order, propriety or solemnity, which is so difficult to be altogether avoided in unpremeditated speech, is far less offensive in a discourse to our fellow-mortals, than in those solemn appeals which we present in their name and our own to the Father of our spirits."

In every Sunday service in this book there is a place for a selection from the Psalms or other Scriptures, to be read alternately by the minister and congregation. This will give variety to the services, which is so much desired by many persons, and will soon make a congregation familiar with these devotional parts of the Scriptures. When we consider that many Sunday-Schools of non-liturgical churches are now using introductory and closing exercises, largely responsive, the tendency of which is to create a taste for a *church* service in which they can take some part besides singing, is it not well to provide suitable forms for them?

I have thought it well, therefore, to submit some forms of Responsive Services, in the belief that there is an increasing desire to have public worship so ordered that the people may have a larger part in it.

If this book shall contribute to the more dignified and orderly worship of God; or shall induce some layman to hold public services where there is no church nor minister; or shall lead some man or men to make a better book—the writer will be devoutly thankful.

PHILADELPHIA, 1885.

CONTENTS.

First Sunday—Morning Service 7
" " —Afternoon or Evening Service.. 13
Second Sunday—Morning Service.............. 18
" " —Afternoon or Evening Service.. 24
Third Sunday—Morning Service.............. 30
" " —Afternoon or Evening Service.. 38
Fourth Sunday—Morning Service............. 43
" " —Afternoon or Evening Service.. 49
Fifth Sunday—Morning Service.............. 55
" " —Afternoon or Evening Service . 59
Sixth Sunday—Morning Service 64
" " —Afternoon or Evening Service.. 72
Seventh Sunday—Morning Service.............. 77
" " —Afternoon or Evening Service.. 84
Eighth Sunday—Morning Service.............. 90
" " —Afternoon or Evening Service.. 94
Ninth Sunday—Morning Service.............. 99
" " —Afternoon or Evening Service.. 104
Tenth Sunday—Morning Service.............. 110
" " —Afternoon or Evening Service.. 119

SPECIAL SERVICES.

An Order for the Baptism of Children.......... 126

An Order for the Baptism of Adults............ 130

An Order for the Admission of Members to the Church................................... 135

An Order for the Administration of the Lord's Supper 136

An Order for the Administration of the Lord's Supper to the Sick........................ 148

An Order for the Marriage Service.............. 155

An Order for the Burial Service of a Child...... 160

An Order for the Burial Service of an Adult.... 167

AN ORDER OF WORSHIP.

FIRST SUNDAY.

Morning Service.

Let us pray.

O GOD, whom heaven and the heaven of heavens cannot contain, but who dwellest with humble and contrite hearts, look in thy mercy upon us who are here assembled, to offer up our sacrifice of prayer and praise unto thee.

Almighty and most merciful Father, we acknowledge and confess before thy holy majesty that we are sinners, conceived and born in guilt and corruption, prone to do evil, who, by reason of our depravity, transgress without end thy holy commandments. Wherefore we have drawn upon ourselves by thy just sentence, condemnation and death. Nevertheless, O Lord, with heartfelt sorrow we repent and deplore our offences; and we condemn ourselves and our evil ways with a true repentance, beseeching that thy grace may relieve our distress.

Be pleased, therefore, to have compassion upon us, O most gracious God! Father of all mercies; for the sake of thy Son, Jesus Christ, our Lord and only Redeemer. And, in removing our guilt and pollution, set us free; and grant us the daily increase of thy Holy Spirit; to the end that, acknowledging from our hearts our unrighteousness, we may be touched with a sorrow that shall work true repentance, and that this may mortify all our sins, and thereby bear the fruit of holiness and righteousness that shall be well-pleasing to thee, through Jesus Christ, our Lord and only Saviour.

(*In unison.*)

Our Father, who art in heaven, hallowed be thy name. Thy kingdom come. Thy will be done in earth, as it is in heaven. Give us this day our daily bread. And forgive us our debts, as we forgive our debtors. And lead us not into temptation, but deliver us from evil. For thine is the kingdom, and the power, and the glory, forever.
            Amen.

SELECTION FROM THE PSALMS.

LESSON FROM THE OLD TESTAMENT.

HYMN.

LESSON FROM THE NEW TESTAMENT.

HYMN.

Let us pray.

O GOD, who hast given the Holy Scriptures to be a light unto our feet and a lamp unto our path, guide our steps at all times in the way of thy precepts. Suffer us not to go astray from thee, nor to err from thy truth. Acknowledging our ignorance and the deceitfulness of our hearts, we call upon thee, O God, for help and deliverance.

O Lord, our merciful Father, be pleased to guide and defend us in all our ways, that we may be delivered in all dangers and temptations of this day, and may so follow the example and pattern which thy dear Son hath left us, both in joyfully bearing and constantly performing thy holy will, that we may glorify thy name, and may abide in thy love.

O Lord God Almighty, who makest all things work together for good to them that love thee, we pray that thou wouldst so order the course of thy providence respecting us, and so enlighten and purify our souls, that all the events of this life may be made conducive to our eternal salvation.

Almighty and most merciful Father, who workest in thy children both to desire and to perform those things that please thee, grant us grace that we may pursue our several callings and duties in the world with a devout, holy, and heavenly mind, considering that we are ever in thy presence and under thine eye; that in all our works and labors, working the work of God, and laboring for the meat that endureth unto everlasting life, we may be found good and faithful servants, and may finally enter into the joy of our Lord.

O God, everlasting and almighty, who art the Creator and Preserver of all men, and who willest not that any should perish, but that all should come to repentance, send forth thy light and thy truth among all nations.

Guide all thy flocks in the paths of truth, righteousness and peace, and make them to be numbered with thy saints in glory everlasting.

Comfort the afflicted; send consolation and joy to all that are in trouble and sorrow; hear the groaning of the prisoners; deliver the oppressed from him that hurteth him; relieve the wants of the poor, and save all afflicted people. Arise, O God, for judgment, and save all the meek of the earth.

O God, who hast revealed to us the light of thy gospel and called us into the fellowship of thy Son, grant that we may put away all the works of darkness, and may walk in purity, uprightness and truth; that we may have fellowship with thee, for thou art light, and in thee there is no darkness at all; that so, when the shadows of this mortal life are passed away, we may behold those things which the eye of man hath not seen, and be made partakers of everlasting glory; through Christ, our Lord.

Almighty and most gracious God, look in compassion upon our infirmities, and uphold us by thy mighty power. Let us not faint or be weary in running the race that is set before us, but, animated by thy promises, may we be strong both to do and endure thy holy will, looking unto our merciful High-Priest, Jesus Christ, who himself suffered and was tempted, and is able to succor us when we are tempted.

We pray that thou wouldst grant a spirit of wisdom and judgment to the President of the United States, to all magistrates, judges, and others invested with authority, that we, under them, may lead a quiet and peaceable life in godliness and honesty, adorning the doctrine of God our Saviour.

And let thy blessing be upon all conditions of men among us. Bless them in the work of their hands; prosper their honest industry; grant unto them the things that are needful for the body and the life that now is; above all, make them rich towards God and heirs of thine everlasting kingdom.

We pray for our kindred, our friends, and all whom thou hast made the instruments of thy grace and bounty to us, that thou wouldst reward and bless them abundantly; and also for our enemies, if we have them, that thou wouldst grant them repentance, and enable us to forgive them from the heart, through Jesus Christ, our Lord.

(*Special or extemporaneous Prayer.*)

HYMN.

SERMON.

Let us pray.

ALMIGHTY and Eternal God, who dost so heartily desire our salvation, and dost so faithfully warn us in manifold ways to think in earnest on the things that belong to our peace; we pray thee to give us thy good Spirit, that we may believe in thy great love and faithfulness with our whole hearts, and may not trifle away our time of grace, but follow thy voice which bids us come to thee while it is yet to-day; for the sake of thy dear Son, Jesus Christ, our Lord.

Amen.

HYMN AND DOXOLOGY.

BENEDICTION OR ASCRIPTION.

FIRST SUNDAY.

Afternoon or Evening Service.

Let us pray.

O LORD, our heavenly Father, who hast commanded us not to forsake the assembling of ourselves together, be pleased to sanctify and bless our meeting together at this time; and grant that, by thy Spirit, our minds may be enlightened, our hearts cleansed, and our wills directed to keep thy holy commandments; through Jesus Christ our Redeemer.

We confess our sins before thee, O God, thou righteous Judge to whom all things are known. We have done evil in thy sight, transgressing thy law, which is holy, just and good; and we are verily guilty before thee; but thou art faithful and just to forgive us our sins and to cleanse us from all unrighteousness.

Justify us freely by thy grace, through the redemption that is in Christ Jesus; that, having our hearts sprinkled from an evil conscience, we may serve thee in holiness and righteousness all our days, through our Lord and Saviour Jesus Christ. May we hear his voice; may we know the doctrine which he hath taught us; may we render a willing obedience to his precepts; may we follow his example; and, finally, may we receive those exceeding great and precious promises which he hath given us. Grant this, we beseech thee, O Lord, through Jesus Christ, who is our Prophet, our Priest, and our King.

(*In unison.*)

Our Father, who art in heaven, hallowed be thy name, etc.

SELECTION FROM PSALMS.

LESSON FROM THE SCRIPTURES.

HYMN.

Let us pray.

O GOD, whose word is quick and powerful, grant unto us who are here before thee, that we may receive thy truth into our hearts in 'faith and love, and so be prepared for every good word and work, to the honor of thy name.

Be pleased, almighty and most gracious God, to increase our faith, hope and charity, our patience, fortitude and meekness, our zeal and diligence in thy service. May we, through thy grace, mortify all sinful affections, resist and subdue all evil habits and abound in every good work. Let our good resolutions be ripened into acts and habits of holiness and virtue, that we may be as epistles of Christ, thy laws being written in our hearts and upon our whole lives; that we may walk worthy of our high calling and adorn the doctrine of God our Saviour.

Dwell in our hearts, we pray thee, O Lord God, and make us temples of thy Holy Spirit; that whereas in ourselves we are weak, corrupt and mortal, we may through thee be strengthened and sanctified; and finally, having obtained the victory over death, may reign in immortal life.

Gracious God, who hast sent thy Son into the world, that whosoever followeth him might not walk in darkness, grant, we beseech thee, that thy gospel may speedily be preached among all nations, so that all flesh may see thy salvation.

O God, everlasting and almighty, whose grace hath appeared, bringing salvation to all men, teach us to deny ungodliness and worldly lusts, and to live soberly, righteously and godly in this present world, looking for the blessed hope, even the glorious appearing of the great God and our Saviour Jesus Christ, who gave himself for us that he might redeem us from all iniquity.

And we beseech thee, O Lord, who hast built thy Church upon the foundation of the apostles and prophets, Jesus Christ himself being the chief corner-stone, to grant a spirit of wisdom and power to thy servants who are appointed to labor in the sacred ministry; that by their doctrine and example thy people may be built up in their holy faith, and sinners may be converted unto thee. And everywhere let thy Word have free course and be glorified; through him who is the Apostle and High-Priest of our profession, Jesus Christ.

Father of mercies, look down in compassion upon the sick and afflicted, upon the poor, the miserable, and the dying, upon the friendless, the despairing, and the tempted; and upon all who are in danger, necessity or tribulation. Send them comfort and deliverance, O God; and do thou, who makest all things work together for good to them that love thee, sanctify their pains and sorrows to the health and salvation of their souls in the day of our Lord Jesus Christ.

We beseech thee, O God, to bless all men; bring them to the knowledge and obedience of the truth. Break thou the arm of the oppressor everywhere, and scatter the counsels of the people that delight in war, and in all the earth let thy kingdom come, which is righteousness and peace and joy in the Holy Ghost, through Jesus Christ our Lord.

(*Special or extemporaneous Prayer.*)

HYMN.

SERMON.

Let us pray.

O LORD, have mercy upon us; and grant that we may receive thy truth into good and honest hearts, and may bring forth the fruit of good living, to the honor of thy great name.

O God, who hast given the day to man for labor, and the night for rest, protect us by thy watchful providence during the coming night, and all the nights and days of our pilgrimage. And when our days are ended, and our work is finished in this world, may we depart hence in the blessed assurance of thy favor, and in the certain hope of the resurrection to immortal life, which thou hast given us in our Lord and Saviour Jesus Christ. Amen.

HYMN AND DOXOLOGY.

BENEDICTION OR ASCRIPTION.

SECOND SUNDAY.

Morning Service.

Let us pray.

ALMIGHTY GOD, the Maker of all things visible and invisible, our Creator and Preserver, who hast sent thy Son to bring us near and make us sons of God, and heirs of eternal life; grant unto us thy grace and blessing, as we are here assembled to offer up our common supplications to thee, to confess our sins, and to render thanks unto thy name for thy great goodness.

May we put away all heedlessness and irreverence, all vain thoughts and distracting cares; and may we draw near to thy presence with earnest, humble, and faithful hearts, in the spirit of holiness. And let our worship and service, being offered in the name and spirit of thy Son, be acceptable to thee, and profitable to us; through him who is our Mediator and Advocate, Jesus Christ.

We confess before thee, O God, our Heavenly Father, that we are sinners; for we have transgressed thy holy laws in thought, word, and deed. We have not loved thee with all our hearts; neither have we loved our neighbors as ourselves. We have loved the world, and the things that are of the world, and have not set our affection on things above, or laid up our treasure in heaven, where Christ, our risen Lord, sitteth at thy right hand.

Almighty God, Father of our Lord Jesus Christ, who hast in thy gospel proclaimed remission of sins to all them that believe in the name of thy Son, and repent of their transgressions against thee; confirm us, we beseech thee, in the faith and hope of this thy promise; and so work in us by thy Holy Spirit, that we may embrace and hold fast thy truth in a pure conscience unto the end, and also may bring forth fruits meet for repentance; that being justified freely by thy grace, and walking continually in the way of thy commandments, we may glorify thy holy name, and may know that we are indeed thy children, and heirs of the kingdom which thou hast promised to them that love thee.

(*In unison.*)

Our Father, who art in heaven, hallowed be thy name, etc.

SELECTION FROM THE PSALMS.

LESSON FROM THE OLD TESTAMENT.

HYMN.

LESSON FROM THE NEW TESTAMENT.

HYMN.

Let us pray.

O GOD, who desirest not sacrifice, and hast no delight in burnt-offering, but has showed us what is good; and who requirest of us to do justly, to love mercy, and to walk humbly with thee, grant us, we pray thee, true repentance; and so direct and govern our hearts and lives that we may render a constant and unfeigned obedience to thy holy laws; that, offering to thee the sacrifices of righteousness, we may be accepted in thy sight, and may obtain our petitions, through Jesus Christ our Lord.

O God, thou King eternal, immortal, invisible, may we, who cannot see thee with the eye of flesh, behold thee steadfastly with the eye of faith, that we faint not under the many temptations and afflictions of this mortal life, but endure as seeing thee who art invisible; that when we shall have done and suffered thy will upon the earth, we may behold the vision of God in heaven, and be made partakers of those unspeakable joys which thou hast promised to them that love thee, through Jesus Christ our Lord.

O God, our bountiful Benefactor, we thank thee for the bread that perisheth, and for all the good things of this present life. May we receive them with gratitude, and enjoy them with temperance and charity. But man liveth not by bread alone. Make us to hunger and thirst after righteousness; that our souls may at length be satisfied with the fulness of thy truth and grace; through him who is the bread of life, and who giveth life unto the world, Jesus Christ our Lord.

Most gracious God, who didst send thy Son into the world to die for our sins, and to rise again; grant that we may rise with Christ to newness of life; abounding in godliness, justice, charity, and meekness; in purity and temperance; in fortitude, patience and resignation; that we may be indeed followers of Christ in all the steps of his blessed and holy life; and may walk worthy of our high calling; through him who is our Redeemer and Lord, and who suffered for us in the flesh, leaving us an example that we should follow his steps.

God of all grace and consolation, send into our hearts thy Holy Spirit to abide with us forever; that we, being taught and quickened, purified and strengthened, by thy heavenly grace, may faithfully and joyfully serve thee all our days; through Christ our Lord.

Blessed Lord, whose will it is that all men should be saved, and who hast commanded us to make intercessions and prayers for all men; we offer up to thee our supplications for the whole human race, that they may be brought to the knowledge and obedience of the truth; for all thy people, that they may fight the good fight and lay hold on eternal life; and may so run the race that is set before them that in due time they may obtain the prize: and for all the afflicted, that it may please thee to sanctify, uphold, and comfort them, and to redeem their souls from all evil.

Look down from the height of thy sanctuary, O merciful Father, upon the sick, the dying, and the bereaved; upon widows and orphans; upon the despairing and the tempted. Lord, have mercy upon them, and upon us also, for we are all of like passions, and compassed about with infirmities. Grant unto us to be humble, sober, and watchful, that we may stand in the evil day. We pray for our kindred, friends, and benefactors, that thou wouldst enrich them with thy favor, and grant unto them a portion in thy heavenly kingdom: and for our enemies, if there are such; that thou wouldst forgive them, and enable us to forgive them from the heart; that, rendering good for evil, we may be indeed thy children.

O God, thou King of glory, who rulest all the nations of the world, and to whom pertain all might, majesty, and dominion in heaven and earth, we beseech thee to regard with thy favor the President of the United States, the Governor of this Commonwealth, all magistrates and judges, and all persons invested with authority. Grant unto them a spirit of wisdom and of the fear of the Lord; and may we, and all under them, lead a quiet and peaceable life in godliness and honesty, showing forth thy praise.

O God, by whose gracious providence we enjoy the good things of this present life, and also all things pertaining to godliness and the life eternal, we, thy unworthy servants, unite in rendering thanks and praise unto thy great name.

Enable us, we entreat thee, O Lord, to manifest our gratitude by a willing and constant obedience to thy righteous commands, and by walking, at all times, after the example of Him whom thou didst send into the world to take away our sins, and make us sons of God, and heirs of immortal life, through Jesus Christ our Lord.

(Special or extemporaneous Prayer.)

HYMN.

SERMON.

Let us pray.

ALMIGHTY and eternal God, who hast graciously bestowed on us the clear light of thy truth, whereby we, notwithstanding our sins, can attain through Christ a childlike trust in thee; we humbly pray thee give us thy Holy Spirit, that we may trust thee with our whole hearts, and may deny ourselves, and bear the cross after thy dear Son in steadfast patience, through Jesus Christ our Lord. Amen.

HYMN AND DOXOLOGY.

BENEDICTION OR ASCRIPTION.

SECOND SUNDAY.

Afternoon or Evening Service.

Let us pray.

ALMIGHTY and everlasting God, who hast promised that in all places where thou dost record thy name thou wilt meet with thy servants and bless them, fulfil to us at this time thy promise, and make us joyful in thy house of prayer.

Enlighten and purify our minds: raise our hearts to thee: endow us with wisdom and understanding: may we know, believe, and love thy truth; and let the words of our mouths and the meditations of our hearts be acceptable in thy sight, O Lord, our strength and our Redeemer.

Lord, have mercy upon us; for we daily sin against thee, transgressing thy holy laws, failing of the duty thou requirest of us, and grieving thy Spirit of grace. Through Jesus Christ thy Son, who ever liveth in thy presence in heaven, our High-Priest and Mediator, be pleased, O Lord, merciful Father, to blot out all our offences, our ignorances and negligences, our unfaithfulness in thy service, our sloth and pride, our love of the world, and all our secret faults and presumptuous sins, by which we have been disobedient unto thy heavenly calling, and have merited thy just displeasure. If thou shouldst enter into judgment, we could not stand; but there is mercy with thee that thou mayest be feared.

(*In unison.*)

Our Father, who art in heaven, hallowed be thy name, etc.

SELECTION FROM THE PSALMS.

LESSON FROM THE SCRIPTURES.

HYMN.

Let us pray.

WE offer unto thee, O Lord, our sacrifice of prayer and praise; we give thee thanks for the mercies of the day, and we commit ourselves, for the night that is coming, to thy gracious protection. Glory be to thee for the day of rest and worship, for the sacred hours which have passed over us, and for all we have enjoyed of Christian fellowship, sympathy, and communion. A day in thy courts is better than a thousand; we would rather be doorkeepers in the house of our God than dwell in the tents of wickedness. Often in the high services of thy church hast thou put joy and gladness into our hearts. May the influence of the Sabbath go with us throughout all the week; may our worldly engagements be regulated and sanctified by religious faith, so that whatever we do may be done as to God.

Blessed Lord, who hast sent thy Son Jesus Christ to die for our sins, and also, by his heavenly doctrine and holy life, to lead us in the paths of truth and righteousness, grant us thy Holy Spirit to dwell in our hearts, to guide our lives, and to sanctify us wholly in body, soul, and spirit; that having glorified thee upon the earth and finished the work thou hast given us to do, we may obtain the victory over all our enemies, and reign in immortal life; through Jesus Christ.

O thou great Master and Lord, who art calling us to serve thee that we may be free, and art intrusting thy talents to our keeping for a season, grant us to be wise and faithful stewards even in that which is least. May we not abuse or bury thy gift, but improve it to thy glory; that when the Lord shall reckon with us, we may be found of him in peace, and may enter into the joy of our Lord.

O God, who hast given us the promise of thy heavenly rest, may we labor earnestly to enter into it. Quicken, we pray thee, our faith and hope. Teach us to mortify whatever in us is earthly, carnal and corrupt. Putting off the works of darkness, may we be clothed with truth, righteousness and purity, and walk as Christ walked.

O God, grant thy blessing upon all pastors and teachers, that they may fully know and faithfully declare thy holy gospel; that the whole church may grow in faith and charity and patience, and may abound in every good word and work.

And we humbly entreat thee, most merciful

God, to receive graciously the sacrifices of praise and prayer which thy people offer unto thee this day throughout the world. Let the cry of thy family come before thee, O Father, and send unto thy children an answer of peace; through our elder brother Jesus Christ.

O Lord, who art from everlasting to everlasting, who knowest the end from the beginning, and who hast given to thy Son the heathen for his inheritance, hasten, we entreat thee, the coming and kingdom of Christ. Let all the ends of the earth remember and turn to the Lord; let all the kindreds of the nations worship before thee. And do thou, who holdest the hearts of all men in thy hand, open a great door and effectual for the preaching of thy servants, that their sound may go into all the earth, and their words to the ends of the world.

O Lord, who art very pitiful and of tender mercy, who art the father of the fatherless and the husband of the widow, and who dost not willingly afflict or grieve the children of men, we lift up our hearts unto thee on behalf of all our brethren who are in any affliction or distress. Look down from thy holy habitation upon the poor and destitute; upon the bereaved and the sorrowful, the sick and the dying; upon those that are in pain and anguish; and upon all that are desolate and oppressed. Send them speedy help and deliverance, O thou Judge of the earth, and so enrich the souls of all thy afflicted servants with patience and hope, that their present trouble may conduce to their eternal salvation; and may they receive in due time the end of their faith; through our merciful High-Priest Jesus Christ, who suffered and was tempted and is able to succor all who are tempted.

Lord of all power and might, we call upon thee whose mercies are from everlasting. We are ignorant, weak and perverse: leave us not, O God, neither forsake us. Guide us with thy counsel; uphold us by thy power. Suffer us not to go astray from thy ways; let us not be weary in well-doing. May we live in thy fear all the days of our life; may we die in thy favor, and let our portion be among thy saints at the glorious appearing of our Lord and Saviour Jesus Christ.

(*Special or extemporaneous Prayer.*)

HYMN.

SERMON.

Let us pray.

O GOD, our heavenly Father, suffer not the good seed of thy truth to be caught away by the wicked one out of our hearts, neither let it be scorched of tribulation or persecution; not be choked with cares and pleasures of this life; but, being received into good and honest hearts, may it bring forth abundantly the fruits of faith and good works, to the glory of thy grace.

O Lord God, in whose presence there is no darkness, for thou dwellest forever in light, keep and defend us and all thy people, in soul and body, during the coming night, and in all the darkness of this mortal life. May we rest in the assurance of thy favor; in the peace of a good conscience; in the hope of a better life; in the faith of thy providence and protection; and in the love of thy Spirit. May we rise up again to diligence in our several callings, to work the work of God while the day lasts, seeing the night cometh in which no man can work. And, whether we wake or sleep, may we live together with Christ.

Lighten our darkness, we beseech thee, O Lord; and by thy great mercy defend us from all perils and dangers of this night; for the love of thy only Son, our Saviour, Jesus Christ. Amen.

HYMN AND DOXOLOGY.

BENEDICTION OR ASCRIPTION.

THIRD SUNDAY.

Morning Service.

Let us pray.

O GOD, accept, we beseech thee, our sacrifice of praise and prayer; and, though we are not worthy to approach thy presence, or to ask anything of thee, do thou receive us graciously, through our great High-Priest and Advocate Jesus Christ.

Almighty God, we render thanks unto thy great name that we have been preserved to see another of the days of the Son of man upon earth. For the sun and the light, for the succession of night and day, and summer and winter, and seed-time and harvest, and the ordinances of heaven; for thy fatherly care and goodness to us the children of men; for thy watchful providence and unspeakable mercy, we magnify thy name, O Lord.

O God, Maker and Governor of the world, who on the seventh day didst rest from all thy works, and hast promised an everlasting rest to all thy faithful servants, make us to rest from our works, that we who are weary and heavy laden with our sins and sorrows may take up the yoke and burden of Jesus Christ, and so find rest unto our souls; for his yoke is easy and his burden is light.

We confess that we are sinners, O God; for we have transgressed thy holy laws, and done despite to thy good Spirit, and walked in counsels of our own. We acknowledge that we have not loved thee with all our heart, nor believed thy faithful word, nor hoped for thy promises, but have been disobedient and rebellious. Neither have we been sober and watchful, nor have we mortified the deeds of the body: but our hearts have been overcharged with cares and pleasures of this life, and we have been too much conformed to the world. Our own hearts condemn us, and thou art greater than our hearts and knowest all things. Forgive us, O Lord, we beseech thee, for Jesus Christ's sake.

(*In unison.*)

Our Father, who art in heaven, hallowed be thy name, etc.

SELECTION FROM THE PSALMS.

LESSON FROM THE OLD TESTAMENT.

HYMN.

LESSON FROM THE NEW TESTAMENT.

HYMN.

Let us pray.

ALMIGHTY GOD, Father of all mercies, we render thanks and praise unto thee for sending thy Son into the world, that he might redeem us from our sin and misery, and make us heirs of everlasting life. May we be justified by faith, and have peace with God, through our Lord Jesus Christ; and grant us thy grace, O Lord, that we may depart from all iniquity, and may be a peculiar people, zealous of good works, showing forth thy praise.

O God, who in the beginning didst cause the light to shine out of darkness, and hast made thy sun to rise again upon the world, shine into our hearts, we pray thee, and deliver us from ignorance and error, from doubt and fear; and so cleanse us by thy Holy Spirit, that we, renouncing the hidden things of dishonesty, and all the works of darkness, may walk before thee in sincerity, purity, and righteousness; that we may have fellowship with thee, and may be followers of him whom thou didst send to be the light of the world, Jesus Christ our Lord.

Almighty and most merciful God, who didst feed thy people of old with manna in the wilderness, teaching us that man liveth not by bread alone, we thank thee for the supply of our daily wants, for the bounties of thy good providence, for life, and breath, and all things: especially for Jesus Christ, thine unspeakable gift, who is the bread of God, coming down from heaven and giving life unto the world.

Guide and strengthen us, O God, with thy truth: refresh our fainting souls with thy promises: animate our hearts, and purify them with thy love; that we may walk with constancy in the way of thy precepts: and having finished our earthly pilgrimage in faith and patience, may we at length be delivered from the toils and dangers of the wilderness, and enjoy forever thy heavenly rest; through him who is the author and finisher of our faith, Jesus Christ our Lord.

O God, omnipotent and everlasting, whose eternal providence is over all thy works, so that a sparrow falleth not to the ground without thee, and even the hairs of our head are numbered; we beseech thee to help and deliver us, in all time of our trouble and adversity, and also in all time of our prosperity; that we be not overwhelmed with despondency and fear, nor lifted up with presumption and pride; but enjoying thy bounties with humility and thankfulness, and bearing thy chastening with faith and hope, we may endure unto the end.

O eternal God, who didst speak unto thine ancient people, out of the midst of thick darkness, with thunderings and lightnings and terrible majesty, we thank thee for thy grace and truth which are now revealed unto us by Jesus Christ thy Son, whom thou hast sent forth, in the fulness of time, to redeem us; that we might no more be servants, in bondage to the world, but might be sons and heirs of God, through him. Send into our hearts, we entreat thee, the spirit of thy Son. Inspire us with perfect love, which casteth out fear; that we may draw near to thy throne of grace, at all times, with true hearts, in full assurance of faith; and having served thee in peace and joy all the days of our life, may at length be made partakers of thy heavenly inheritance: through our great High-Priest, who is passed into the heavens, Jesus the Son of God.

Grant unto us grace, we beseech thee, Almighty God, that as thou hast taught us thy will, so we may at all times choose and obey thy holy laws; making our light to shine before men, to the glory of thy name.

Almighty God, who hast made of one blood all nations, and whose will it is that all men should come to the knowledge of the truth and be saved, send the light of thy gospel into all lands, and pour out thy Spirit upon all flesh; that thy name may be hallowed everywhere, and thy kingdom may come, which is righteousness and peace, and joy in the Holy Ghost.

Build up thy holy temple in the earth, and fill it with thy glory. Adorn and beautify thy church with the graces of thy Spirit, that every member of the same may be unto honor and praise at the appearing of our Lord Jesus Christ.

Relieve the sick and the destitute; comfort the sorrowful; draw nigh, in thy mercy and grace, to the dying; and let all the miserable find consolation and redemption in thee, O God.

Defend and prosper our country. Let the people be obedient to thy holy laws, living godly, righteous, and sober lives, to the glory of thy name. Give grace to thy servant the President of the United States, to the governor of this State, and to all magistrates, judges, and rulers; to all classes and conditions of men; that we may all fulfil our appointed tasks as under the eye of the great Master, and may in due time enter into the joy of the Lord.

Almighty and most merciful Father, we, thy unworthy creatures, unite in giving thanks and praise unto thy name for thy great goodness and mercy to us and to all men. We acknowledge thee, O Lord, as the bountiful giver of all the good things of this present life, but especially of that blessed hope of an everlasting inheritance, which thou hast given us in Jesus Christ our Lord. From this time henceforth may we consecrate ourselves to thy service in all things; living as those who are not their own, being bought with a price, through Jesus Christ our Lord.

(Special or extemporaneous Prayer.)

HYMN.

SERMON.

Let us pray.

WE praise and bless thy holy name, Father of mercies and God of all grace, that thou hast had compassion upon us sinners; that thou didst send thy Son to seek and save us; that he took on him the form of a servant, and the likeness of sinful flesh, and fulfilled thy law, and was obedient to all thy will, even unto death: that he made propitiation for our sins; and that when he had overcome the sharpness of death, he opened the kingdom of heaven to all believers; that he sitteth at thy right hand in glory everlasting; that he will come again in majesty to judge the quick and the dead; and will reign till all enemies are put under his feet; that he is our advocate with thee, the captain of our salvation, the author and finisher of our faith; that he is our light, and life, and hope; that he is touched with the feeling of our infirmities, having been in all points tempted as we are; that he ever liveth to make intercession, and saveth to the uttermost them that come unto thee by him: that thou hast sent unto us thy Holy Spirit, and the gospel of thy grace; and hast permitted us in peace and safety to enjoy another of the days of the Son of man upon the earth, to unite with thy people in calling upon thy name, and learning the way of eternal life; through our Lord and Saviour Jesus Christ. Amen.

HYMN AND DOXOLOGY.

BENEDICTION OR ASCRIPTION.

THIRD SUNDAY.

Afternoon or Evening Service.

Let us pray.

ALMIGHTY and most merciful Father, we thank thee that we are permitted to approach thy throne of grace through Jesus Christ, the great High-Priest of our profession; assured that thou hearest prayer, and that thou wilt bestow upon us all things needful, whether for the body or the soul, for the life that now is, and that which is to come.

If we say that we have no sin, we deceive ourselves, and the truth is not in us. If we confess our sins, thou art faithful and just to forgive us our sins, and to cleanse us from all unrighteousness.

O God, thou searcher of hearts, in whom there is no darkness, and from whom our sins cannot be covered, we humble ourselves before thy holy majesty; we confess that we have been foolish, rebellious, deceived. We have been unthankful for thy mercies, distrustful of thy promises, disobedient to thy commands, and by our great wickedness have provoked thee to cast us off from thy favor and fellowship. Behold, we return unto thee, our God, from whose ways we have so grievously departed, and implore thy pardon for all our sin and folly. Forgive us, we beseech thee; forgive thy people, whom thou hast redeemed with the most precious blood of thy dear Son; create in us clean and contrite hearts, and grant unto us thy heavenly grace, that we turn not again unto folly; and help us heartily to forgive others, as we beseech thee to forgive us, and to serve thee henceforth in newness of life, to the glory of thy holy name; through Jesus Christ our Lord.

(*In unison.*)

Our Father, who art in heaven, hallowed be thy name, etc.

SELECTION FROM THE PSALMS.

LESSON FROM THE SCRIPTURES.

HYMN.

Let us pray.

O LORD GOD, who didst proclaim thy law from Mount Sinai in terrible majesty, we give thee thanks that the thunder, and the earthquake, and the fire are now past, and that we can hear the still small voice of thy grace speaking to us in the gospel.

Deliver us, O Lord, from the spirit of bondage and fear, and shed abroad thy love in our hearts by the Holy Ghost; that we may serve thee in peace and joy, hoping for thy glorious promises, through Jesus Christ our Saviour.

We praise and bless thy holy name, Father of mercies, and God of all grace, that thou hast had compassion upon us, miserable sinners:

That thou didst send thy Son to seek and save us:

That he took on him the form of a servant, and the likeness of sinful flesh, and fulfilled thy law, and was obedient to all thy will even unto death:

That he made propitiation for our sins; and when he had overcome the sharpness of death, he opened the kingdom of heaven to all believers:

That he sitteth at thy right hand in glory everlasting:

That he will come again in glory and majesty to judge the quick and the dead, and will reign till all his enemies are put under his feet:

That he is our Advocate with thee; the Captain of our salvation; the author and finisher of our faith:

That he is touched with the feeling of our infirmities; having been, in all points, tempted as we are:

That he ever liveth to make intercession for us; and saveth to the uttermost them that come unto thee by him:

That thou hast sent unto us the gospel of thy grace; and hast permitted us to unite with thy people in calling upon thy name, and learning the way of eternal life.

O God, who dwellest from eternity in light that is inaccessible and full of glory, we thank thee that thou hast revealed thyself unto us, so dispelling our ignorance, and guiding our steps in the ways of righteousness and peace.

Incline our hearts, we beseech thee, to hear his voice who speaketh to us from heaven; to obey and follow him who is the light of the world; that, being translated out of the kingdom of darkness, and redeemed from all the power of sin and death, we may receive thy promises, and be made partakers of glory, honor, and immortality; through our Lord and Redeemer, Jesus Christ.

Almighty God, the Creator and Preserver of all mankind, we pray thee to send forth into all lands the light of thy truth; and grant that all men may receive it in faith and love, that they may be saved.

We commit ourselves and all that are dear to us, our kindred, friends and benefactors, and those who have desired to be remembered in our prayers, to thy mercy and grace, and to the keeping of thy good providence, O Lord our God. Grant unto them and us that which is needful for the present life, and with it bestow thy blessing. Enrich us with patience and resignation, with cheerfulness and fortitude.

Cleanse our souls with the inspiration of thy Holy Spirit: adorn them with the ornaments of thy grace: sanctify us wholly in body, soul, and spirit; and preserve us blameless to the coming and kingdom of our Lord.

(*Special or extemporaneous Prayer.*)

HYMN.

SERMON.

Let us pray.

LET thy gospel, O Lord, come to us not in word only, but in power and in the Holy Ghost; that we may be guided into all truth, and also be strengthened unto all obedience and enduring of thy will; that we may abound in the work of faith, and the labor of love, and the patience of hope, and so may be made meet to be partakers of thy heavenly inheritance; through Jesus Christ our Lord.

Lighten our darkness, we beseech thee, O Lord; and by thy great mercy defend us from all perils and dangers of this night; for the love of thy only Son, our Saviour Jesus Christ. Amen.

HYMN AND DOXOLOGY.

BENEDICTION OR ASCRIPTION.

FOURTH SUNDAY.

Morning Service.

Let us pray.

WE bow before thy Divine Majesty, O God, adoring thee, the Lord of heaven and earth; of whom, and through whom, and to whom are all things; to whom be ascribed all might, majesty, and dominion, world without end.

All things are of thee. The heavens declare thy glory: the earth is full of thy riches: so also is the great and wide sea. The day is thine: the night also is thine: thou hast prepared the light and the sun: thou hast set all the borders of the earth: thou hast made summer and winter. Who would not fear thee, O Lord, and glorify thy name? for thou only art holy.

O God, who art exalted above all blessing and praise, and needest not our service, for all things in heaven and earth are thine; grant that we, and all our brethren throughout the world, may worship thee this day in spirit and in truth, and may find acceptance with thee, through our Advocate and Mediator Jesus Christ.

(*In unison.*)

Our Father, who art in heaven, hallowed be thy name, etc.

SELECTION FROM THE PSALMS.

LESSON FROM THE OLD TESTAMENT.

HYMN.

LESSON FROM THE NEW TESTAMENT.

HYMN.

Let us pray.

WE humble ourselves in the dust before thee, O Lord, confessing our sins. Our hearts and lives are sinful. Thy fear hath not been at all times before our eyes; neither have we loved thee with all our hearts, nor studied to serve and glorify thee.

O thou who art more ready to hear than we are to pray, and art wont to give more than either we desire or deserve, pour down upon us the abundance of thy mercy; forgiving us those things of which our conscience is afraid, and giving us those things which we are not worthy to ask, but for thy mercy's sake, through Christ our Lord.

Deliver us from all the temptations of the world, the flesh, and the devil. Take not thy grace from us; let us never want thy help in our need, or thy comforts in the day of our danger and calamity. Try us not beyond our strength, nor afflict us beyond our patience, nor smite us but with a Father's rod. Thou art our rock and our strong salvation. Deliver us, O God, from the miseries of this world, and save us from the wrath to come. Rescue us from the evils we have done, and preserve us from the evils we have deserved.

Receive us who approach the throne of thy grace, in the name of Jesus Christ. Give unto each of us that which is best for us: cast out all sin from within us: work in us a fulness of holiness, of wisdom, and spiritual understanding; and make us fruitful in every good work; that, living before thee with undefiled bodies and sanctified spirits, we may be presented without spot and blameless at the coming of our Lord Jesus Christ and all his saints.

O God, who hast commanded us to watch and pray that we enter not into temptation, endue us with sobriety, vigilance, and godly fear. Leave us not to our own weak and deceitful hearts; neither let us be turned aside by the power of evil example; but may we put on the whole armor of God, that we may stand in the evil day. Succor us, O heavenly Father, in our time of trial and temptation, through thy Holy Spirit, by whom thy Son our Lord was led into the wilderness to be tempted of the devil; that, our conflict ended, angels may be sent to minister unto us, as heirs of that salvation which thou hast promised to as many as obey and follow him.

O God, Father of mercies, we thy unworthy

servants unite in giving thanks and praise unto thee for all the goodness and grace which thou hast showed unto us and all men. Thou didst create us in thy own image; thou hast preserved us by thy good providence; thou hast delivered us from dangers and from death; thou hast kept our feet from falling; our eyes from tears; thou hast bountifully supplied our wants, and loaded us with benefits: above all, we magnify thy great name in that thou didst send thy Son into the world, that we might not perish by reason of our sins, but be made heirs of everlasting life.

Sovereign Master and Lord of the world, we commend to thy protection and favor the powers that be established to rule the nations; especially thy servant the President of the United States. Grant thy grace to all that bear rule over us. Qualify and dispose them to govern in wisdom and righteousness; and may their administration be so blessed of thee, that the whole people may have peace and prosperity.

O Lord, our gracious God, we implore thy mercy for all who may be in peril by sea or land; for widows and orphans; for the poor; for prisoners; for the bereaved, the sick, and the dying, and for all the afflicted and sorrowful. May it please thee, merciful Father, to look upon them in thy compassion, to strengthen, comfort, and deliver them; and finally receive their spirits into thy rest, and crown them with heavenly glory.

Finally, O Lord, we beseech thee to pour out thy blessing upon us, our persons, our families, and all our concerns and interests. Give us whatever is needful for this present life, and also for that which is to come; and deliver us from vain regrets, needless anxieties, and unbelieving fears. We are in thy hand; we commit ourselves to thee; thou wilt not leave us nor forsake us. May we be diligent and prudent in our several callings; and may they yield fruits to the supply of our need, to the comfort of our brethren, and to thy glory. Let us not place our good in riches, pleasures, honors, or any of the things of this perishing world; but in thy favor, in the peace and joy of thy Spirit, and in the hope of everlasting life, which thou hast promised to them that love thee.

Mercifully receive our prayers, and send us an answer in peace; through thy well-beloved Son, our Lord and Saviour, Jesus Christ.

(Special or extemporaneous Prayer.)

HYMN.

SERMON.

Let us pray.

O LORD, let our prayers come before thee in the name of Him who is the Angel of the everlasting covenant, who alone is worthy to receive all the glory of our redemption; and for whose sake we entreat thee to bless us and keep us this day, and all the days and nights of our life on earth; and when the golden bowl shall be broken, and the spirit shall return to thee, may it be to each of us the commencement of a life of glory that shall never know an end. Amen.

HYMN AND DOXOLOGY.

BENEDICTION OR ASCRIPTION.

FOURTH SUNDAY.

Afternoon or Evening Service.

Let us pray.

O LORD our God, we lift up our eyes unto the hills from whence cometh our help. Our help cometh from the Lord. Thou only art the Fountain of life and peace, and in thy presence is fulness of joy. Father in heaven, from whom cometh down every good and perfect gift, grant us thy blessing, and incline thine ear unto us, as we come before thee in the sacred services of thy house. Merciful Saviour, who sittest at the right hand of the Father and makest intercession for us, fulfil now thy promise: "Where two or three are gathered together in thy name, there am I in the midst of them." O Holy Ghost, the Comforter, help our infirmities and enable us to worship in the beauty of holiness; through Christ our Lord.

(*In unison.*)

Our Father, who art in heaven, hallowed be thy name, etc.

SELECTION FROM THE PSALMS.

SCRIPTURE LESSON.

HYMN.

Let us pray.

O GOD, Father of our Lord Jesus Christ, of whom the whole family in heaven and earth is named, give unto us who now draw near to thy presence thy heavenly grace, that we may worship thee with contrite, faithful and obedient hearts; and grant that we may be accepted in thy sight and may receive our petitions; for we present them before thee in his name, who is the great High-Priest of our profession, our Mediator and Advocate, Jesus Christ.

Almighty and everlasting God, Creator of the world, Father of angels and men, have mercy upon us.

Thou blessed and only Potentate, who dwellest in thick darkness, though thou thyself art light without darkness; incomprehensible, inscrutable; who seest all things, thyself unseen; who knowest all, though thou canst not be known; have mercy upon us.

Lord God, most merciful and gracious, who daily loadest us with benefits and art good even to the unthankful and the evil, have mercy upon us.

Thou didst breathe into us thy Spirit; thou didst create us in the image of God, making us only a little lower than the angels and putting all things under our feet; but the crown is fallen from our head, for we have rebelled against thee; have mercy upon us, for thou knowest our frame: thou rememberest that we are dust.

We have sinned, we have done wickedly, departing from the living God; transgressing in thought, word and deed thy most righteous laws, and resisting thy Holy Spirit; therefore we cry unto thee: Lord, have mercy upon us.

Before thee, the Judge of the world and the Searcher of hearts, whose eyes behold the evil and the good, and to whom all things are naked and open, we do confess our sins, and acknowledge our great iniquity; O Lord, we entreat thee, have mercy upon us.

Our heavenly Father, who didst send forth thy Son, in the fulness of time, to bring near thy salvation, grant unto us repentance and remission of sins, according to the riches of thy grace; and bless us by turning every one of us away from all iniquity.

O God, who quickenest all things, Lord and Giver of life, who didst bring again from the dead our Lord Jesus, that great Shepherd of the sheep, quicken us, thy people and sheep of thy pasture, with divine and heavenly life; inspire us with faith, hope, charity, patience, and all the fruits of the Spirit, that we may glorify thee upon the earth, may edify and strengthen our brethren, may work out our own salvation, may grow in grace, and be faithful unto death; that in due time we may be presented faultless before the presence of thy glory with exceeding joy, and receive that crown of righteousness which thou hast promised to them that love thee.

In all time of our adversity; in our sickness, pain, and fear; in perplexity and distress; when we suffer wrongfully; and in all time of our trial and temptation: have mercy upon us.

In our health and wealth; in our ease, prosperity, and honor; and when all men speak well of us, Lord, have mercy upon us.

In the joys and sorrows, and in all the changes of this mortal life; at the hour of death, and in the day of judgment: have mercy upon us.

O God, let it please thee not to cut us down as cumberers of the ground; but spare us, and so quicken us by thy grace, that we may live no longer unto ourselves, but unto him who died for us and rose again, and whom thou hast exalted at thy right hand, that he may be Lord both of the dead and of the living.

(*Special or extemporaneous Prayer.*)

HYMN.

SERMON.

Let us pray.

O LORD our heavenly Father, our days and weeks glide swiftly away, reminding us of the end of our days, and the night which is at hand, when we shall cease from all our earthly cares and labors, and lie down in the dust in silence and darkness.

May we, by thy grace, so redeem the time that we shall close our eyes upon this world without sorrow or fear, and sleep in Jesus, resting in hope of thy promises; that when the day of God shall dawn, we may rise with joy, and put on immortality, being redeemed from all the power of corruption, and made like unto the Son of God; that we, with all thy saints, may live and reign with him; who died for us and rose again, and ever liveth and reigneth with thee the Father, in the unity of the Eternal Spirit, world without end.

O thou who dwellest in light, keep us thy servants, and all that are dear to us, during the darkness and silence of the night that is coming, from all evil, whether of the body or the soul; for thou only knowest our dangers, and thou only canst defend and save us. And when the night and darkness of this life are passed away, grant that we may awake and behold the light of thine eternal glory in the kingdom of heaven; through him that loved us, and hath redeemed us from darkness, sin, and death, Jesus Christ our Lord. Amen.

HYMN AND DOXOLOGY.

BENEDICTION OR ASCRIPTION.

FIFTH SUNDAY.

Morning Service.

Let us pray.

O THOU who hast made the church thy dwelling-place, and hast taught us in thy word not to forsake the assembling of ourselves together, regard in special mercy, we beseech thee, thy servants, who meet this day in thy holy courts. Manifest thyself unto us as thou dost not unto the world, and so bless unto us all these means of grace, that our worship may prepare us both to serve thee now, and to glorify thee hereafter, in thine eternal kingdom.

(In unison.)

Our Father, who art in heaven, hallowed be thy name, etc.

SELECTION FROM THE PSALMS.

LESSON FROM THE OLD TESTAMENT.

HYMN.

LESSON FROM THE NEW TESTAMENT.

HYMN.

Let us pray.

O GOD, who dost instruct us by the Holy Scriptures, as we are now met together to read, hear, and meditate upon them; enlighten our minds and purify our hearts, that we may be able to comprehend, and receive as we ought, the things which are therein revealed to us. Make thy truth effectual by thy Holy Spirit, that the good seed may be received into our hearts, as into a soil well prepared, and may bring forth fruit with abundance; that we may not only hear thy word but keep it, living in accordance with its divine instructions all the time of our sojourn in this world, so that we may come, finally, to eternal salvation, through Jesus Christ our Lord.

O Lord our God, eternal and almighty, we acknowledge and confess that we are sinners; born in iniquity, prone to evil; unable of ourselves to do that which is good; transgressing daily, and in many ways, thy holy commandments, and by thy just judgment deserving of condemnation and death. But, O Lord, we are deeply grieved for having offended thee. We condemn both ourselves and our sins with unfeigned penitence. We seek refuge in thy mercy, and humbly entreat thee to help us.

Be pleased then, O most gracious God, Father of mercies, to have compassion on us, and for the sake of Jesus Christ thy Son, to pardon all our sins. Grant unto us also, and increase in us from day to day, the grace of thy Holy Spirit, that acknowledging and bewailing more and more our iniquities, we may renounce them with all our hearts, and may bring forth the fruits of holiness and righteousness, which are well-pleasing in thy sight; through Jesus Christ our Lord.

We thank thee that thou hast made us after thine own image; that thou hast spared us hitherto, and hast brought us to the worship of thy holy name; that thou hast preserved us safe amidst the changes of this mortal life, and hast supplied our wants out of thy fulness. But especially do we bless thee for sending thy Son Jesus Christ into the world to lighten our darkness, and lead us unto heavenly truth. We bless thee for his holy incarnation, for his life on earth, for his sufferings and death upon the cross, for his resurrection from the dead, for his glorious ascension to thy right hand, whence he shall come again to judge the quick and the dead. We thank thee for the giving of the Holy Ghost, for the sacraments and ordinances of thy Church, for the communion of saints, for the forgiveness of sins, for the resurrection of the body, and for the life everlasting.

(Special or extemporaneous Prayer.)

HYMN.

SERMON.

Let us pray.

ALMIGHTY GOD, Father of all mercies, we, thine unworthy servants, do give thee most humble and hearty thanks, for all thy goodness and lovingkindness to us, and to all men. We bless thee for our creation, preservation, and all the blessings of this life; but above all, for thine inestimable love in the redemption of the world by our Lord Jesus Christ; for the means of grace, and for the hope of glory. And, we beseech thee, give us that due sense of all thy mercies, that our hearts may be unfeignedly thankful, and that we may show forth thy praise, not only with our lips, but in our lives; by giving up ourselves to thy service, and by walking before thee in holiness and righteousness all our days; through Jesus Christ our Lord, to whom, with thee and the Holy Ghost, be all honor and glory, world without end.
Amen.

HYMN AND DOXOLOGY.

BENEDICTION OR ASCRIPTION.

FIFTH SUNDAY.

Afternoon or Evening Service.

Let us pray.

O GOD, light of the hearts that see thee, and life of the souls that love thee, and strength of the thoughts that seek thee; from whom to be turned away is to fall, to whom to be turned is to rise, and in whom to abide is to stand fast forever: grant us now thy grace and blessing, as we are here assembled to offer up our common worship.

We confess unto thee, Father Almighty, Lord of heaven and earth, our sins which we have committed against thee, and against the law of Christ. We confess unto thee the wickedness of our hearts, out of which have proceeded all manner of evil thoughts and acts, and we are without excuse before thee. But especially, O God, we bewail those things which are the present burden of our heart and conscience. For all our sins and transgressions, our iniquities and offences, which Thou bringest to our remembrance, we cast ourselves upon thy mercy; and those which, through ignorance or carelessness, through foolishness, or the sinful darkness of our heart, we remember not, but which thou, who knowest all secrets, seest that we have committed against thee, do thou forgive; and do thou cleanse us from them all, for thy mercy's sake, O Lord. And accept our confession, and make our repentance sincere, through Jesus Christ.

(*In unison.*)

Our Father, who art in heaven, hallowed be thy name, etc.

SELECTION FROM THE PSALMS.

LESSON FROM THE SCRIPTURES.

HYMN.

Let us pray.

ALMIGHTY GOD, our heavenly Father, we render thee hearty thanks that thou hast permitted us once more to enter the courts of thy sanctuary, to hear thy word, to sing thy praise, to enjoy the communion of saints, and to be built up in our most holy faith on the foundation of the apostles and prophets. Continue to us the use of the precious means of grace, and grant that we all who are now assembled in thy sanctuary on earth, may be numbered with the saints in glory everlasting, and may render praise unto thee, the Father, the Son, and the Holy Ghost, God blessed for evermore.

O God, by whom, through whom, and in whom, all things live, which live truly and blessedly; pity and help us, according as thou knowest we need, in body and in soul; that being freed from the chains with which we are bound, and casting off all that entangles us, we may serve thee alone, cleave to thee alone, and direct every effort toward thee alone, who knowest all things, and canst perform all things, and who livest for evermore.

God of all comfort, we commend to thy mercy all whom thou art pleased to visit with any cross or tribulation; the nations that are afflicted with famine, pestilence, or war; those of our brethren who suffer persecution for the sake of the gospel; all in danger by sea or by land, and all persons oppressed with poverty, sickness, or any other distress of body or sorrow of mind. We pray particularly for the sick and afflicted, and for any who desire to be remembered in our prayers (*and for any such known to ourselves, whom we now name in our hearts before thee*). May it please thee to show them thy fatherly kindness, and to deliver them out of all their troubles; above all, grant them the consolations of which they have need, dispose them to patience and resignation, and make their afflictions promote the salvation of their souls.

O God, regard with thy favor this worshipping assembly. Accept our worship, notwithstanding its imperfections; and grant that henceforth, putting all our trust in thy well-beloved Son, enlightened by his teaching, guided by his example, and sanctified by his Spirit, we may walk in newness of life, and so be prepared for that blessed life which thou hast promised to thy children in heaven.

Hear us, O merciful Father, in these our supplications, for the sake of thy dear Son Jesus Christ, our Lord; to whom, with thee and the Holy Ghost, be all honor and glory, world without end.

(Special or extemporaneous Prayer.)

HYMN.

SERMON.

Let us pray.

O GOD, who dost instruct us by thy Holy Scriptures, we beseech thee, enlighten our minds and purify our hearts, that we may be able to comprehend, and receive as we ought, the things which are therein revealed to us. Assist thy servants that they may proclaim thy truth with purity, clearness, and simplicity. Make their teaching effectual by the power of the Holy Spirit, that the good seed may be received into our hearts, as into a soil well prepared, and may bring forth fruits with abundance; that we may not only hear thy word but keep it; so that living in accordance with its divine instructions all the time of our life in this world, we may come finally to eternal salvation, through Jesus Christ our Lord.

Lighten our darkness we beseech thee, O Lord; and by thy great mercy defend us from all perils and dangers of this night for the love of thine only Son our Saviour Jesus Christ. Amen.

HYMN AND DOXOLOGY.

BENEDICTION OR ASCRIPTION.

SIXTH SUNDAY.

Morning Service.

(The reader may begin the service by reading one or more of the following passages:)

How beautiful upon the mountains are the feet of him that bringeth good tidings, that publisheth peace; that bringeth good tidings of good, that publisheth salvation; that saith unto Zion, thy God reigneth!

Thou wilt keep him in perfect peace, whose mind is stayed on thee: because he trusteth in thee.

Trust ye in the Lord for ever: for in the Lord Jehovah is everlasting strength.

Wherewith shall I come before the Lord, and bow myself before the high God? shall I come before him with burnt offerings, with calves of a year old?

Will the Lord be pleased with thousands of rams, or with ten thousands of rivers of oil? shall I give my first-born for my transgression, the fruit of my body for the sin of my soul?

He hath showed thee, O man, what is good; and what doth the Lord require of thee, but to do justly, and to love mercy, and to walk humbly with thy God?

Let us pray.

O GOD, who didst speak in times past unto the fathers by the prophets, and hast in these last days spoken to us by thy Son from heaven, give us, we pray thee, humble, teachable, and obedient hearts, that we may receive what he hath revealed, and do always what he hath commanded. And as man liveth not by bread alone, but by every word of God, grant that we may ever hunger after this heavenly food, that it may be to us sweeter than honey, and more to be desired than gold, and that we may find in it daily provision on our way to eternal life.

(*In unison.*)

Our Father, who art in heaven, hallowed be thy name, etc.

(*Then may be said or sung the Gloria Patri; or a Hymn may be sung.*)

Glory be to the Father, and to the Son, and to the Holy Ghost:

As it was in the beginning, is now, and ever shall be, world without end. Amen.

(*In unison.*)

I believe in God the Father Almighty, Maker of heaven and earth:

And in Jesus Christ his only Son our Lord; who was conceived by the Holy Ghost, born of the Virgin Mary; suffered under Pontius Pilate, was crucified, dead, and buried; the third day he rose from the dead; he ascended into heaven, and sitteth on the right hand of God the Father Almighty; from thence he shall come to judge the quick and the dead.

I believe in the Holy Ghost; the holy Catholic Church—the communion of saints; the forgiveness of sins; the resurrection of the body; and the life everlasting. Amen.

HYMN.

LESSON FROM THE OLD TESTAMENT.

SELECTION FROM THE PSALMS.

LESSON FROM THE NEW TESTAMENT.

Let us pray.

O LORD, our heavenly Father, Almighty and everlasting God, who hast safely brought us to the beginning of this day, defend us in the same with thy mighty power, and grant that this day we fall into no sin, neither run into any kind of danger; but that all our doings may be ordered by thy governance, to do always that which is righteous in thy sight, through Jesus Christ our Lord. Amen.

Most gracious Father, forgive, we humbly beseech thee, our many and grievous transgressions. Take from us all impurity of thought or desire;

all envy, pride, and hypocrisy; all falsehood and deceit; all covetousness, vain-glory, and indolence; all malice and anger; and everything that is contrary to thy will.

O Lord, make clean our hearts within us.

Save us, O Lord God, from ingratitude towards thee, from an evil use of thy fatherly gifts, from mistrust of thy divine Providence, from impatience and despondency, from immoderate care for temporal things, and from neglect of those things which are eternal.

Save us, O Lord.

Remember, we beseech thee, thine ancient mercies; and though we have not shown the love and duty of children, yet look on us with the compassion of a Father.

Hear us, O Lord; for our trust is in thee.

Enlighten our understandings, that we may discern the wonders of things visible and invisible, the secret ways of thy Spirit, the order of thy Providence, the new life that is the light of men, and the dayspring of eternal hope.

Hear us, we beseech thee, O Lord.

Take us as a living sacrifice, that our bodies may be servants to our spirits, and both our bodies and our spirits be thy servants.

Show us the path of life, O Lord.

Teach us what thou wouldst have us to do; and uphold us by thy mighty power, that every work of ours may begin always from thee, and by thee be happily ended. Shed abroad thy love in our hearts, that we may love thee above all things, and our neighbor as ourselves, and by that charity which never faileth, be abundantly refreshed in our toils and sufferings.

Show us the path of life, O Lord.

Give thy law unto this nation, O thou Creator of the ends of the earth, who appointest to the nations their place; and deeply plant its liberty and sanctity in the hearts of all among us; and let its fruits be seen in the wisdom and uprightness of our magistrates and legislators; in the high gifts and godly devotedness of our teachers of truth and righteousness; and in the honest industry, sobriety, and mutual respect of all our people.

O Lord, lift up the light of thy countenance upon us.

Lay open our souls alike to thy bounty and thy discipline. If thy rain cherisheth the grass, and thy sunshine ripeneth the grain, make us glad with the joy of gratitude. If the fruit tree should not blossom, and the fields should yield no grain, if the flock should be cut off from the fold, and there should be no herd in the stalls, still would we rejoice in thee, and love thee not only for thy gifts, but for thyself.

Be thou, O Lord, our portion forever.

Sanctify the ties that bind us to friends and kindred; and so fill us with love, gentleness, and forbearance, that we may walk in our homes with a perfect heart, and have joy in each other which passeth not away.

O God, thou infinite one, abide in us.

May parents bring up their children in the nurture and admonition of the Lord; and children love and reverence their parents. Stir up in the young a zeal for whatever things are pure and true and good, that they may fearlessly witness for thee, and be ready, for righteousness' sake, to share the reproach of Christ. And keep the heart of the aged fresh with sweet affections and a quiet trust; that, at their eventide there may be light, and they may rest in hope of thine everlasting day.

O God of our lives, bind us more closely to thyself.

Let thy supporting presence be felt by those who are in need, sickness, or any adversity: even though they be utterly destitute of man's aid, yet let the comfort of thy Holy Spirit never depart from them: give them patience and constancy, and in thine own good time turn their sorrows into joy.

Hear us, O Lord, and let our prayers come before thee.

We praise and thank thee, O God, for all thy faithful servants who have departed this life: mercifully grant, we beseech thee, that we, being compassed about with so great a cloud of witnesses, may lay aside every weight, and the sin which doth so easily beset us, and run with patience the race that is set before us; looking unto Jesus, the author and finisher of our faith.

Hear us, we beseech thee, O Lord.

O Lord, bless all the faithful laborers who strive to be fellow-workers with thee; more and more may they widen the fellowship of Christ, and bring nearer the promise of thy kingdom; till they fulfil the angels' song, "Glory to God in the highest, on earth peace, and goodwill to men."

O Lord, the world is thine; cleanse it for thyself with the water of life.

(*Special or extemporaneous Prayer.*)

HYMN.

SERMON.

Let us pray.

O MERCIFUL GOD, the Father of our Lord Jesus Christ, who is the Resurrection and the Life, in whom whosoever believeth shall live though he die, and whosoever liveth and believeth in him shall not die eternally; we meekly beseech thee, O Father, to raise us from the death of sin unto the life of righteousness; that when we shall depart this life, we may rest in him; and that at the general resurrection in the last day, we may be found acceptable in thy sight, and receive that blessing which thy well-beloved Son shall then pronounce to all that love and fear thee, saying, "Come ye blessed children of my Father, inherit the kingdom prepared for you from the foundation of the world." Grant this, we beseech thee, O merciful Father, through Jesus Christ, our Mediator and Redeemer. Amen.

HYMN AND DOXOLOGY.

BENEDICTION OR ASCRIPTION.

SIXTH SUNDAY.

Afternoon or Evening Service.

We will come into thy house in the multitude of thy mercy; and in thy fear will we worship toward thy holy temple.

Let the words of our mouths, and the meditations of our hearts, be acceptable in thy sight, O Lord, our strength and our Redeemer.

Let us pray.

ALMIGHTY and most merciful Father, we have erred and strayed from thy ways like lost sheep; we have followed too much the devices and desires of our own hearts; we have offended against thy holy laws; we have left undone those things which we ought to have done, and we have done those things which we ought not to have done, and there is no health in us. But thou, O Lord, have mercy upon us, miserable offenders; spare thou those, O God, who confess their faults; restore thou those who are penitent, according to thy promises declared unto mankind in Christ Jesus our Lord; and grant, O most merciful Father, for his sake, that we may hereafter live a godly, righteous and sober life, to the glory of thy holy name. Amen.

(*In unison.*)

Our Father, who art in heaven, hallowed be thy name, etc.

HYMN.

LESSON FROM THE OLD TESTAMENT.

SELECTION FROM THE PSALMS.

LESSON FROM THE NEW TESTAMENT.

Let us pray.

ALMIGHTY GOD, the fountain of all holiness, who by thy Word and Spirit dost conduct all thy servants in the way of peace and righteousness, inviting them by thy promises, winning them by thy long-suffering, and endearing them by thy loving-kindness; grant unto us so truly to repent of our sins, so carefully to reform our errors, so diligently to watch over all our actions, so industriously to perform all our duty, that we may never willingly transgress thy holy laws: but that it may be the work of our lives to obey thee, the joy of our souls to please thee, the satisfaction of all our hopes and the perfection of all our desires to live with thee, in the holiness of thy kingdom of grace and glory; through Jesus Christ our Lord.

Visit and cleanse our consciences, we beseech

thee, O Lord, that when thy Son Jesus Christ shall come he may find us ready for his appearing, not sleeping in our sins, but awake and rejoicing in his salvation.

Quicken us to work the works of him that hath sent us, while it is day, because the night cometh wherein no man can work; and what we do, enable us to do it heartily, as unto the Lord, and not unto men.

O Lord God, who givest to men the blessed hope of eternal life by our Lord Jesus Christ, and hast promised thy Holy Spirit to them that ask him; be present with us, and with all thy people, in the dispensation of thy holy Word; and grant that our worship, being offered in the name and in the spirit of thy Son, may be acceptable unto thee and profitable unto ourselves; through our only Mediator and Advocate, Jesus Christ our Lord.

We call to mind, O God, before thy throne of grace, all who are near and dear to us, and all for whom we are bound to pray, beseeching thee to remember them for good, and to supply, as may be most expedient for them, all their desires and wants. And we commend to thy mercy all who have wronged us by word or deed, if there be such, beseeching thee to forgive them all their sins, and to bring them together with us to thy heavenly kingdom.

Grant to us thy peace and love, O God our

Saviour, who art the hope of all the ends of the earth.

Crown the years with thy goodness, for the eyes of all wait upon thee.

Remember all thy family of mankind from one end of the earth to the other.

Remember those who remember the poor; give of thy grace heavenly gifts to liberal givers.

Remember all in loneliness, and comfort the mourner with thine own consolations.

Remember every faithful soul in trial, and comfort every one in sorrow and distress.

O Helper of the helpless, bring the wanderer home and give health to the sick.

Strengthen those that are weak in faith and ready to fall.

Gather all those that are scattered, and set them in the living temple of upright and holy men.

Stand forth for the widow and shield the orphan; give a heritage of joy to them that are childless.

Remember, Lord, all that are captive or sick, all that are in prisons and hospitals, all that are restrained of their liberty for their reformation, all that are in affliction, necessity, or emergency everywhere.

Remember all such for good.

And now, Lord, we beseech thee to hear these our prayers, and grant us thy grace that our waiting upon thee at this time may be for thy glory and our good, through Jesus Christ our Lord.

(*Special or extemporaneous Prayer.*)

HYMN.

SERMON.

Let us pray.

ALMIGHTY GOD, who alone canst enable us rightly to apply thy holy word, grant that we may learn from it those lessons which thou didst intend to impart, that so being preserved from all the errors and inventions of men, we may evermore walk in thy light, through Jesus Christ our Lord.

Lighten our darkness, we beseech thee, O Lord; and by thy great mercy defend us from all perils and dangers of this night, for the love of thy only Son, our Saviour Jesus Christ. Amen.

HYMN AND DOXOLOGY.

BENEDICTION OR ASCRIPTION.

SEVENTH SUNDAY.

Morning Service.

The Lord is high above all nations, and his glory above the heavens. Who is like unto the Lord our God, who dwelleth on high, who humbleth himself to behold the things that are in heaven, and in the earth?

We have not an High-Priest that cannot be touched with the feeling of our infirmities; but was in all points tempted like as we are, yet without sin. Let us therefore come boldly unto the throne of grace, that we may obtain mercy, and find grace to help in time of need.

Let us pray.

ALMIGHTY GOD, our heavenly Father, being now assembled to present to thee our praises and our prayers, and to hear thy word; we beseech thee, that, according to the promises which thou hast made to hear us when we call upon thee in the name of thy Son, it may please thee to regard us in thy mercy, and so to raise our thoughts and desires to thyself, that we may this day render to thee an acceptable service; through Jesus Christ our Lord.

(In unison.)

Our Father, who art in heaven, hallowed be thy name, etc.

HYMN.

LESSON FROM THE OLD TESTAMENT.

SELECTION FROM THE PSALMS.

LESSON FROM THE NEW TESTAMENT.

Let us pray.

ALMIGHTY FATHER, who hast given thine only Son to die for our sins, and to rise again for our justification, grant us so to put away the leaven of malice and wickedness, that we may alway serve thee in pureness of living and truth; through the merits of thy Son, Jesus Christ our Lord.

O Lord, who hast taught us that all our doings without charity are nothing worth, send thy Holy Spirit, and pour into our hearts that most excellent gift of charity, the very bond of peace, and of all virtues, without which whosoever liveth is counted dead before thee; grant this for thine only Son, Jesus Christ's sake.

O God, who hast taught us in thy holy Word to be careful for nothing, but in everything, by prayer and supplication with thanksgiving, to make known our requests unto thee, give ear unto our prayer, and attend to the voice of our supplication.

Remember not, Lord, our offences; but spare us, good Lord, spare thy people, and be not angry with us forever,

Spare us, good Lord.

From all evil and mischief; from sin and thoughts of sin; from perplexity and temptation; from thy wrath and from everlasting judgment,

Good Lord, deliver us.

From all impurity of thought and deed; from excess in pleasure and love of gain; and from following a multitude to do evil,

Good Lord, deliver us.

From lightning and tempest; from plague, pestilence, and famine; from battle and murder and untimely death,

Good Lord, deliver us.

From wicked conspiracy and unholy strife; from false doctrine and carelessness in faith; from hardness of heart and contempt of thy divine judgments,

Good Lord, deliver us.

By the dwelling of thy truth in man, by the abounding of thy love in men of low estate, who suffer sorrow and trial;

We beseech thee to hear us, good Lord.

By the agony of them that mourn, by our sorrow at the grave, and by our trust in God our everlasting Saviour;

We beseech thee to hear us, good Lord.

By thy good confession in Pilate's hall, by thine agony and bloody sweat, by thy death of shame, thy cross and passion;

Good Lord, deliver us.

In our trial and our sorrow, in our health and well-being, in all life's changes and chances, in the hour of death, and in the day of judgment;

Good Lord, deliver us.

We sinners do beseech thee to hear us, O Lord God, and that it may please thee to rule and govern thy people everywhere in the right way;

We beseech thee to hear us, good Lord.

That it may please thee to bless all rulers and governors, that they may rule over free nations in true piety and order; and guide all magistrates and judges that they do wrong to no man, but follow justice, equity and right;

We beseech thee to hear us, good Lord.

That it may please thee to illuminate all teachers and preachers of thy truth with right knowledge and understanding of thy word, that both by their preaching and living they may set it forth and show it accordingly;

We beseech thee to hear us, good Lord.

That it may please thee to give us hearts to love and serve thee, and to frame our lives according to thy holy will and commandment,

We beseech thee to hear us, good Lord.

That it may please thee to give to all thy people grace to hear meekly thy word and to receive it in love and bring forth fruits of righteousness;

That it may please thee to bring into the way of truth all such as have erred, and to make the light of thy truth shine upon them that sit in darkness;

That it may please thee to strengthen them that do stand; to comfort the weak-hearted; to raise up the fallen; to bring back the wandering, and to make our paths free from all perplexity;

That it may please thee to succor, help, and comfort all that are in danger, necessity, and anguish of body and mind;

We beseech thee to hear us, good Lord.

That it may please thee to preserve all that travel by land or by water, all sick persons and young children, and to show thy mercy upon all prisoners and captives;

That it may please thee to defend and provide for the aged, fatherless, and widowed, and all that are desolate and oppressed;

That it may please thee to forgive our enemies and evil-doers and evil-speakers, and to help us to forgive them, to deliver us from all their snares, and in thy good time to change their hearts;

We beseech thee to hear us, good Lord.

That it may please thee to give largely of thy gifts of the seasons, to preserve for us herb and fruit and harvest, and that with thankfulness we may enjoy them;

We beseech thee to hear us, good Lord.

That it may please thee to give us true and right hearts before thee, to pardon all our sins, negligences, and ignorances, and to give us the grace of thy Holy Spirit to amend our lives according to thy word;

We beseech thee to hear us, good Lord.

O God, that despisest not the sighing of a broken heart nor the desire of the sorrowful, mercifully assist our prayers that we make before thee in all our troubles, trials, and sorrows, whensoever they come upon us; and for the glory of thy name turn from us all those evils that we most justly have deserved; and grant that in all our anxiety, sickness, or weakness we may put our whole trust in thy kindness and faithfulness, and ever serve thee in holiness, patience, and pureness of living, to thy honor and glory, through Jesus Christ our Lord.

(*Special or extemporaneous Prayer.*)

HYMN.

SERMON.

Let us pray.

LORD of all power and might, grant us, we beseech thee, a deep and true insight into thy glorious truth, that being justified by grace and renewed in the spirit of our minds by the indwelling of the Holy Ghost, the Comforter, we may be sanctified for thy service both here and hereafter, and at length enter into the joy of our Lord and Saviour Jesus Christ.

Almighty God, grant us, we pray thee, the spirit

of wisdom and of a sound mind, that in all sobriety and humility we may search the Scriptures, and so be enabled rightly to understand and obey thy will through Jesus Christ our Lord. Amen.

HYMN AND DOXOLOGY.

BENEDICTION OR ASCRIPTION.

SEVENTH SUNDAY.

Afternoon or Evening Service.

The hour cometh, and now is, when the true worshippers shall worship the Father in spirit and in truth; for the Father seeketh such to worship him. God is a spirit; and they that worship him must worship him in spirit and in truth.

O worship the Lord in the beauty of holiness: fear before him all the earth.

Let us pray.

O GOD, our heavenly Father, let thy blessing be upon us as we come together in thy name to worship thee. Thou art not far from us, but so near that thou not only hearest our words, but thou knowest the thoughts of our hearts. Let the words of our mouths and the meditations of our hearts be acceptable in thy sight, O Lord, our Strength and our Redeemer.

(In unison.)

Our Father, who art in heaven, hallowed be thy name, etc.

HYMN.

LESSON FROM THE OLD TESTAMENT.

SELECTION FROM PSALMS.

LESSON FROM THE NEW TESTAMENT.

Let us pray.

ALMIGHTY and most merciful God, we would bow before thee under a deep sense of our unworthiness. We have grievously sinned against thee in thought, word, and deed. We have broken thy laws, we have neglected our duty, we have forgotten thee.

Have mercy upon us, O Lord.

O thou Lamb of God, that takest away the sins of the world, who didst come to seek and to save that which was lost, who art exalted to be a Prince and a Saviour, to give repentance and forgiveness of sins, who hast invited the weary and the heavy laden to come unto thee, that thou mayest give them rest,

Have mercy upon us.

Thou, who art the true light, which lighteneth every man that cometh into the world, who ever livest to make intercession for us, who canst be touched with a feeling of our infirmities, who, because thou thyself wast tempted, art able to succor them that are tempted, and who hast promised that him that cometh unto thee thou wilt in nowise cast out,

Have mercy upon us.

From all our sins and offences; and from the punishment due to them, from hardness of heart and impenitence; and from contempt of God's holy word and commandment; from all fretfulness and impatience; from vanity and pride; from self-indulgence and neglect of others,

Good Lord, deliver us.

From fear of man, and forgetfulness of God; and from the corruptions of our own hearts; from irreverence and indevotion; from profaning the mysteries of religion, and the means of grace; from repining at thy dispensations, from neglect of thy warnings, and abuse of thy mercies,

Good Lord, deliver us.

From an angry and haughty spirit; from self-confidence and contempt of others; from the love of this present world and all inordinate affections; from neglect of the world unseen;

From terrors of conscience; from the fear of death; from unrepented sin; from our spiritual enemies;

From unpreparedness for death; from distraction and distrust in our last conflict; from the wrath of God and the hiding of his face;

Good Lord, deliver us.

Almighty God, give us thy heavenly grace. Guide us by thy love in our daily work, that all may rightly understand and find profit in the instruction we receive. Grant that we may be faithful and diligent in the tasks appointed us, and give unto us such success as may be best for us. Preserve us, by thy Holy Spirit, from all selfish and unjust conduct, from unruly and unworthy ways, and make us generous and true, pure and honest in all things. May we strive each hour of the day to do what is pleasing in thy sight; so shall we rejoice in thy fear and love. O Lord, let our prayer be acceptable unto thee, through the merits and mediation of Jesus Christ our Saviour.

O Lord, we beseech thee, cleanse our hearts and lips from deceit and guile, and save us from untruthful and double ways. Keep us from murmuring and impatient thoughts, and from all harsh words and deeds, that we may be kind to those around us, tender-hearted and compassionate, slow to take offence, ready to forgive, and cheerful under disappointment and vexation. Be thou our Guide in the midst of distractions, and our Help in time of need. Be thou ever present to protect and comfort us, and, when this life is ended, may we have our portion amongst thy redeemed ones in the kingdom of glory.

O compassionate Saviour, who during thy life on earth didst magnify thyself chiefly in showing mercy and pity, and who didst go about doing good to the souls and bodies of the sinful and suffering; grant us, we pray thee, such a measure of thy spirit that we may find our chief pleasure in doing good to all around us. Give us tender hearts and willing hands, that we may do thy work in sustaining the weak, raising them that fall, and comforting the sad and sorrowing. Teach us all that we are brethren, and heirs of the kingdom which thou hast promised to them that love thee. Keep us from all words and deeds which may offend, or lead astray; and grant to us, at the last, the joy of hearing that in doing good to the least of thy little ones we did it unto thee.

May the Lord Almighty order all our ways and doings in his peace; may he direct and rule our hearts in all things, and bring us to life everlasting, for Jesus Christ's sake.

(*Special or extemporaneous Prayer.*)

HYMN.

SERMON.

Let us pray.

ALMIGHTY GOD, our heavenly Father, we beseech thee to bless to us thy word which we have heard this day. Give us clear views of thy truth and of our duty to thee and to our fellow-men. And if anything has been said which is especially adapted to our needs, we pray thee to impress it on our hearts and consciences. Continue to us the means of grace, and help us to make the best improvement of them, and grant that we all may be numbered with thy saints in glory everlasting, and so praise thee, the Father, the Son, and the Holy Ghost, for ever and ever. Amen.

Lighten our darkness, we beseech thee, O Lord; and of thy great mercy defend us from all perils and dangers of this night, for the love of thy only Son, our Saviour Jesus Christ. Amen.

HYMN AND DOXOLOGY.

BENEDICTION OR ASCRIPTION.

EIGHTH SUNDAY.

Morning Service.

(The reader may recite the following :)

We will come into thy house in the multitude of thy mercy, and in thy fear will we worship toward thy holy temple.

Let the words of my mouth and the meditations of my heart be acceptable in thy sight, O Lord, my Strength and my Redeemer.

Let us pray.

O ALMIGHTY GOD, from whom cometh down every good and perfect gift, pour out upon us the spirit of grace and supplications; deliver us from coldness of heart and wanderings of mind, that, with steadfast thoughts and kindled affections, we may worship thee in spirit and in truth; through Jesus Christ our Lord.

(In unison.)

Our Father, who art in heaven, hallowed be thy name, etc.

HYMN.

LESSON FROM THE OLD TESTAMENT.

SELECTION FROM THE PSALMS.

LESSON FROM THE NEW TESTAMENT.

Let us pray.

ALMIGHTY GOD, Searcher of all hearts, in whom there is no darkness, from whom our sins cannot be covered, we would humble ourselves before thee. We confess that we have been foolish and rebellious. We have been unthankful of thy mercies, we have been distrustful of thy promises, we have been disobedient of thy commands, we have provoked thee. But we would return to thee, our Father, from whom we have so grievously departed; we would implore thy pardon for all our sin and folly. Forgive us, we beseech thee. Create in us clean hearts and give us thy heavenly grace, that we may not turn again to folly, but may serve thee henceforth in newness of life; through Jesus Christ our Lord.

Give ear, O Lord, unto our prayer, and attend to the voice of our supplication.

Give us, we beseech thee, those blessings which thou hast promised to all who truly love and serve thee.

O Lord, make us poor in spirit, that ours may be the kingdom of heaven.

Make us to mourn for sin, that we may be comforted by thy grace.

Make us meek, that we may inherit the earth.

Make us to hunger and thirst after righteousness, that we may be filled.

Make us merciful, that we may obtain mercy.

Make us pure in heart, that we may see God.

Make us peacemakers, that we may be thy children.

Make us willing to endure persecution for righteousness' sake, that our reward may be in heaven.

O God, by whom all things live which live truly and blessedly, pity and help us according to our need, that being freed from the bonds of sin and casting off all that entangles us, we may serve thee and cleave to thee through Jesus Christ our Lord.

O God, our heavenly Father, grant, we beseech thee, that, knowing the uncertainty of life, we may constantly depend upon the coming of thy Son, our Saviour Jesus Christ, and that in that blessed hope we may watch and be sober, exercising true godliness and working out our own salvation with fear and trembling, so that with all thy saints we may be presented holy and unblamable before the presence of thy glory with exceeding joy, through him that loved us and washed us from our sins in his own blood, Jesus Christ our Lord.

O God, whose word is quick and powerful, grant unto us who are here before thee, and to thy people everywhere, thy Holy Spirit, that we may receive thy truth into our hearts in faith and love. May it teach and guide and uphold and comfort us, so that, being no longer children in understanding, we may grow to the stature of perfect men in Christ Jesus, prepared for every good word and work to the honor of thy name through Jesus Christ our Lord.

(Special or extemporaneous Prayer.)

HYMN.

SERMON.

Let us pray.

O GOD, who hast prepared for them that love thee such good things as pass man's understanding, enable us so to distinguish between the teaching of the Divine Spirit and the conclusions therefrom of erring and sinful men, that, abiding in the simplicity of the gospel, we may be preserved from all error. Deliver us, we beseech thee, from everything tending to weaken the authority of thy holy word, that, so resting evermore under the shadow of thy wing, our souls may be kept in perfect peace; through Jesus Christ our Lord. Amen.

HYMN AND DOXOLOGY.

BENEDICTION OR ASCRIPTION.

EIGHTH SUNDAY.

Afternoon or Evening Service.

(The reader may begin the service with one or more of the following sentences:)

I WILL arise and go to my Father, and will say unto him, Father, I have sinned against heaven and in thy sight.

Like as a father pitieth his children, so the Lord pitieth them that fear him.

If any man sin, we have an advocate with the Father, Jesus Christ the righteous.

Let us pray.

O GOD, who dost instruct us by thy Holy Scriptures, we beseech thee, enlighten our minds and purify our hearts, that we may be able to comprehend, and receive as we ought, the things which are therein revealed to us. Assist thy ministers that they may proclaim thy word with purity, clearness, and simplicity. Make their preaching effectual by the virtue of the Holy Spirit, that the good seed may be received into our hearts, as into a soil well prepared, and may bring forth fruits with abundance; that we may not only hear thy word but keep it, so living in accordance with its divine instructions all the time of our sojourn in this world that we may come finally to eternal salvation, through Jesus Christ our Lord.

(*In unison.*)

Our Father, who art in heaven, hallowed be thy name, etc.

HYMN.

LESSON FROM THE OLD TESTAMENT.

SELECTION FROM THE PSALMS.

LESSON FROM THE NEW TESTAMENT.

Let us pray.

ALMIGHTY GOD, unto whom all hearts are open, all desires known, and from whom no secrets are hid, cleanse the thoughts of our hearts by the inspiration of thy Holy Spirit, that we may perfectly love thee, and worthily magnify thy holy name; through Christ our Lord.

We come before thee, under a deep sense of our unworthiness and guilt. We have grievously sinned against thee in thought, in word, and in deed; we have come short of thy glory; we have broken thy commandments, and turned aside every one of us from the way of life, and in us there is no soundness nor health.

Forgive us the sins of our past lives and remember not the evil thoughts and unlawful desires of our hearts, the idle and wicked words of our lips, the sinful deeds and fruitless actions of our lives.

O Lord, in all these things have mercy upon us.

Forgive our neglect of thy mercies, the hardness of our hearts at thy goodness, and the forgetfulness of thy chastisements.

O Lord, in all these things have mercy upon us.

From the evils of this present world, from the evil of sin in the world to come, and from the false freedom of an undisciplined life,

Good Lord, deliver us.

From pride and covetousness, from slander, vain-glory, and hypocrisy, from the great guilt of tempting others to sin, from the unhappiness of being ourselves perverted, from ignorance of thy will and neglect of what we know to be our duty, from denying thee before men for worldly ends, from the temptations to which by nature we are most exposed, and from going back into any sins of which we have repented,

Good Lord, deliver us.

We sinners do beseech thee to hear us, and pray that thou wouldst defend and preserve thy Church in true religion, and give the blessing of peace and order to all Christian people.

We beseech thee to hear us, O Lord.

That thou wouldst give us thy Holy Spirit with the pardon of all our sins, and grace to persevere unto the end; that thou wouldst enlarge our hearts with true charity one toward another, that we may feed the hungry, clothe the naked, comfort the distressed, and do good to every one according to our means,

We beseech thee to hear us, O Lord.

That thou wouldst give to us thy grace always to remember the end of our creation, the vanity of the world, the shortness of our life, the certainty of our death, and the misery of such as die in their sins,

We beseech thee to hear us, O Lord.

God of all comfort, we commend to thy mercy all who suffer any sorrow, all people afflicted with famine or pestilence or war, all our fellow-men who suffer persecution for the sake of the gospel, all who are in danger by sea or by land, and all persons oppressed with poverty, sickness, or any other distress of body or mind.

O God our Father, regard with thy favor this waiting company. Accept our worship notwithstanding its imperfections, and grant that henceforth, putting all our trust in thy well-beloved Son, we may walk in newness of life, and so prepare for that blessed life which thou hast promised to thy children in heaven.

(*Special or extemporaneous Prayer.*)

HYMN.

SERMON.

Let us pray.

INCLINE our hearts, O Lord, to receive thy word, and so deliver us from the traditions of men and the delusions of sin that we may not be led astray from the simplicity that is in Christ, but, ever abiding under the shadow of thy wing, may be kept from all evil through the merits and mediation of Jesus Christ our Lord.

God of all grace, whom rightly to know is life eternal, grant us so to receive thy Son Jesus Christ as the way, the truth, and the life, that we may steadfastly walk in the way that leadeth to everlasting blessedness; through Jesus Christ our Lord and Saviour.

Lighten our darkness, we beseech thee, O Lord; and of thy great mercy defend us from all perils and dangers of this night; for the love of thy only Son, our Saviour Jesus Christ. Amen.

HYMN AND DOXOLOGY.

BENEDICTION OR ASCRIPTION.

NINTH SUNDAY.

Morning Service.

The sacrifices of God are a broken spirit; a broken and a contrite heart, O God, thou wilt not despise.

Offer the sacrifices of righteousness, and put your trust in the Lord.

Let us pray.

O GOD, the Father of our Lord and Saviour Jesus Christ, the mighty God who art blessed for evermore, we thy people and the sheep of thy pasture, would draw near to thee with reverence and godly fear.

Look down from heaven, in thy tender love, on us approaching thee through thy Son, and sanctify our souls and bodies by thy Holy Spirit, and strengthen us, that our prayers may go up before thee as incense, and be accepted as a sweet savor, through Jesus Christ our Lord.

(In unison.)

Our Father, who art in heaven, hallowed be thy name, etc.

HYMN.

LESSON FROM THE OLD TESTAMENT.

SELECTION FROM THE PSALMS.

LESSON FROM THE NEW TESTAMENT.

Let us pray.

O GOD our Creator, and Redeemer, and Sanctifier,
Hear us and help us.

O thou God and Father of our Lord Jesus Christ, who hast called us with an high and heavenly calling, unto a lively hope by the resurrection of Jesus Christ from the dead,
We praise and adore thee.

O thou, who hast made us in thine own image; who hast redeemed us by thine only Son; who hast called us by thy Holy Spirit; who hast adopted us as thy children; who hast given thine angels charge over us; who hast encompassed us with all blessings;
Have mercy upon us.

O thou, who hast chosen us in thy Son before the creation of the world; who hast called us to the fellowship of thy saints; who hast prepared for us an eternal kingdom;
Have mercy upon us.

O thou, who to save sinners didst take upon thee the nature of man; who wast tempted like as we are, yet without sin; who didst become obedient unto death, even the death of the cross; who by thy precious blood hast cleansed us from all sin;

who didst lie in the grave for our sakes; who didst overcome death, and rise from the dead; who hast ascended into heaven; and who sitteth at the right hand of God the Father Almighty, from whence thou shalt come to judge the quick and the dead;

Have mercy upon us.

O God, the Father of our spirits, from whom no speech nor language estrangeth, dwell and move in the thoughts of all mankind; more and more breathe the spirit of truth and piety into the hearts of all people; and by the secret working of thy righteousness be thou the unity, peace, and concord of all nations.

Shine, O Holy Spirit, upon the darkness of our minds; take from us self-delusion and vain fears; make us steadfast in the path thou clearly showest, and trustful where thou leadest our blind feet. Lift up the weak-hearted, lest they fall; and strengthen the wavering for the victory over temptation.

Hear our prayer, O Lord.

To all the desolate make thyself known as a refuge in the day of trouble; as a defence in danger, and the healer of sorrow; as a Father of the fatherless, and the strength of the lonely. Speak, O Lord, in the silence, to the mourner, the captive, the dying; and leave with them thy peace.

Hear our prayer, O Lord; we wait upon thee.

Forgive our evil thoughts, O Lord; take every

root of bitterness away, and create pure affections in us; that, through good report or evil, our love for each other and for all men may never fail; and that no offences, though they be seventy times seven, may stir us to ill-will, or move us to injure any of our fellow-creatures.

Hear our prayer, O Lord; we wait upon thee.

O God, our heavenly Father, who beholdest thy repenting children from afar, meet and receive us in mercy, sinners as we are.

O God, our heavenly Father, who callest thy wanderers home, in mercy receive us.

O God, who by thy Holy Spirit dost comfort, direct, and sanctify the hearts of thy faithful servants,

In mercy receive us.

If thou require innocency, we are not worthy to be called thy children: yet arise, O Lord, and say that thy love is greater even than our guilt.

O turn us again, and we shall be turned.

We love thy courts, O Lord, and entreat thee to send light and peace into thy sanctuary; to arm thy ministers and people with the sword of the Spirit, and bring all thy worshippers to the obedience and simplicity of Christ.

Hear our prayer, O Lord; we wait upon thee.

Visit our land, O Lord. Let it be the chief joy of our rulers to be servants of thy will; and may all judges execute justice and maintain peace; and dispose all, whether rulers or people, to repair the breaches of ancient wrong, to renew the virtues of our forefathers and perform all the duties of our time.

Hear our prayer, O Lord; we wait upon thee.

(*Special or extemporaneous Prayer.*)

HYMN.

SERMON.

Let us pray.

GRANT unto us, Almighty God, thy peace that passeth understanding; that we, amid the storms and troubles of our life, may rest in thee, knowing that all things are in thee; not beneath thine eye only, but under thy care, governed by thy will, guarded by thy love; so that with a quiet heart we may see the storms of life, the cloud and the thick darkness; ever rejoicing to know that the darkness and the light are both alike to thee. Guide, guard, and govern us even to the end, that none of us may fail to lay hold upon the immortal life, through Jesus Christ our Lord. Amen.

HYMN AND DOXOLOGY.

BENEDICTION OR ASCRIPTION.

NINTH SUNDAY.

Afternoon or Evening Service.

Make a joyful noise unto the Lord, all ye lands.

Serve the Lord with gladness; come before his presence with singing.

Know ye that the Lord he is God; it is he that hath made us, and not we ourselves; we are his people and the sheep of his pasture.

Enter into his gates with thanksgiving and into his courts with praise: be thankful unto him and bless his name.

For the Lord is good; his mercy is everlasting; and his praise endureth to all generations.

Let us pray.

ALMIGHTY GOD, our heavenly Father, we have come together to worship thee, to offer our songs and supplications, and to hear thy holy word. Thou hast promised to hear and answer all who call upon thee in the name of thy Son. We, therefore, beseech thee to look down upon us in mercy; and so purify our thoughts and our affections, that we may render unto thee an acceptable service, through Jesus Christ our Lord.

(In unison.)

Our Father, who art in heaven, hallowed be thy name, etc.

HYMN.

LESSON FROM THE OLD TESTAMENT.

SELECTION FROM THE PSALMS.

LESSON FROM THE NEW TESTAMENT.

Let us pray.

O GOD, who hast given thy Holy Scriptures for our instruction, we beseech thee to enlighten our minds and purify our hearts that we may worthily read, hear, and meditate upon them, and may understand and receive as we ought the things which thou hast revealed. Enable all who speak in thy name to declare thy word with purity and clearness, with simplicity and zeal. Make their teaching effectual through the influence of thy Holy Spirit, so that the good seed may bring forth fruit in abundance. Grant that we may be not only hearers but doers of thy word; and that living as thy children ought to live, we may find everlasting salvation, through Jesus Christ our Lord.

O Lord our God, thou art very great, thou art clothed with honor and majesty. Thou art the King eternal, immortal, invisible, the only wise God.

Thou art the blessed and only potentate, King of kings and Lord of lords.

All the earth shall worship thee.
All the kings of the earth shall praise thee.
They that go down to the sea, and all that is therein, the isles and the inhabitants thereof, shall praise thee.
The heavens praise thee.
All thy servants, those that stand in the house of the Lord, praise thee.
Angels round about thy throne praise thee.
Much people in heaven praise thee.
Let all the people praise thee, O God, let all the people praise thee.
We give thee thanks, O Lord God Almighty, for all thy goodness to us.
For all thy mercies we praise thee, O God.
For food and raiment, for day and night, for the heavens which declare thy glory, and the earth which is full of thy bounty; for the gift of thy Son, for the glorious Gospel of the blessed God, and a good hope through grace,
We praise thee, O God.
O thou that hearest prayer, unto thee shall all flesh come; hear us, for all men; for all that are in authority,
Hear us, O God.
For the poor and the needy, for the fatherless and the widow, that they cast all their care on thee; for the laborer in the field, for those who go down to the sea in ships, and do business in the great waters, for those who buy and sell and

get gain, that they lay up treasure for themselves in heaven,
Hear us, O God.
For the dark places of the earth which are full of the habitations of cruelty, that thy way may be known upon earth, thy saving health among all nations,
Hear us, O God.
Give ear, O Shepherd of Israel, stir up thy strength and come and save us.
Save us, O God of our salvation.
From the works of iniquity, from bloody and deceitful men, from the love of the world, from the lust of the flesh, from a wounded spirit, from the fear of death, and the terrors of the Lord,
Save us, we beseech thee.
Restore unto us the joy of thy salvation and all spiritual blessings in heavenly places in Christ Jesus.
O Lord, restore.
Fellowship with the Father and with his Son Jesus Christ, the glorious liberty of the children of God, the inheritance of the saints in light,
O Lord, restore.
Lord, have mercy upon us.
Son of God, have mercy upon us.
When our heart is overwhelmed within us; in the day of temptation and adversity, in the terrors of the shadow of death, in the day of grief and of desperate sorrow, in the time of old age, in the day of death,

Have mercy upon us.

O thou who takest away the sin of the world—who didst come to seek and to save that which was lost—Lamb of God, our light and life and our peace, put away our sins. Holy and blessed Spirit, our comforter, our teacher, our sanctifier, who didst come down on thy servants in the early days of the church as tongues of fire, fill our hearts with heavenly love, and our lips with words of wisdom, that we may be prepared for thy service in this world, and for thy kingdom and glory in heaven, for Christ's sake.

Holy, blessed, and glorious Trinity, everlasting and gracious Lord, be our portion, our refuge, our deliverer. Make us to be numbered with thy saints in glory everlasting. Save thy people and bless thine heritage. May we be of that holy company who have washed their robes and made them white in the blood of the Lamb. Make us children of light and of the day, and save us now and for ever.

Save us, O merciful God, from all the dangers and calamities to which we may be exposed. Deliver us from all our sins, preserve us from every evil thought, and from all that is contrary to thy holy will. Give unto us at all times good and holy thoughts, pure, meek, and peaceable dispositions, entire resignation to thy providence, fervent love to thee, and sincere charity towards our fellow-men. May we lay up our treasure in heaven, so that watching and praying without ceasing, and leading humble, righteous, and sober lives, we may pass our days in peace, looking for the coming of the Saviour, Jesus Christ our Lord.

(Special or extemporaneous Prayer.)

HYMN.

SERMON.

Let us pray.

O GOD, our heavenly Father, again we thank thee for thy holy word. Make it more and more plain to us, and help us to love it more. And if the things which have now been said are adapted to our wants and circumstances, and if they are in accord with thy teachings, impress them on our hearts. Forgive, we pray thee, the imperfections of our service, and graciously accept us in our worship, through Jesus Christ our Lord.
Amen.

HYMN AND DOXOLOGY.

BENEDICTION OR ASCRIPTION.

TENTH SUNDAY.

Morning Service.

ENTER not into judgment with thy servants, O Lord; for in thy sight shall no man living be justified.

If we say we have no sin, we deceive ourselves, and the truth is not in us. If we confess our sins, thou art faithful and just to forgive us our sins, and to cleanse us from all unrighteousness.

Let us pray.

O GOD, most high and holy, who dwellest in the holy place, make us holy, and bring us near to thee, and cleanse us from all defilement, that we may worship thee, the God of our fathers, for thou art he that blesseth and halloweth all things; through Jesus Christ our Lord.

We have sinned against thee, but thou hast spared us; we have wandered from thee, but thou hast sought us; we were lost, but thou hast saved us. O God our Saviour, thou hast broken our chains, that we might be free; thou hast healed our diseased souls, that we might not perish; thou hast enriched us who were poor, with the treasures of thy salvation; thou hast made us who had nothing, to inherit all things; and even now all things are ours. Therefore, with one heart and with one voice we laud and magnify thy glorious name; and, with thy saints on earth and in heaven, we ascribe blessing, and honor, and glory, and power, unto Him that sitteth upon the throne, and unto the Lamb, forever and forever. Amen.

(In unison.)

Our Father, who art in heaven, hallowed be thy name, etc.

HYMN.

LESSON FROM THE OLD TESTAMENT.

(After which may be said or sung the following hymn:)

WE praise thee, O God; we acknowledge thee to be the Lord.
All the earth doth worship thee, the Father everlasting.
To thee all angels cry aloud; the heavens and all the powers therein.
To thee cherubim and seraphim continually do cry,
Holy, holy, holy, Lord God of Sabaoth;
Heaven and earth are full of the majesty of thy glory.
The glorious company of the apostles praise thee.
The goodly fellowship of the prophets praise thee.
The noble army of martyrs praise thee.
The holy Church throughout all the world doth acknowledge thee,

The Father, of an infinite majesty;
Thine adorable, true, and only Son,
Also the Holy Ghost, the Comforter.
Thou art the King of glory, O Christ.
Thou art the everlasting Son of the Father.

When thou tookest upon thee to deliver man, thou didst humble thyself to be born of a virgin.

When thou hadst overcome the sharpness of death, thou didst open the kingdom of heaven to all believers.

Thou sittest at the right hand of God in the glory of the Father.

We believe that thou shalt come to be our Judge.

We therefore pray thee help thy servants whom thou hast redeemed with thy precious blood.

Make them to be numbered with thy saints in glory everlasting.

O Lord, save thy people and bless thine heritage;
Govern them and lift them up forever.
Day by day we magnify thee;
And we worship thy name ever, world without end.

Vouchsafe, O Lord, to keep us this day without sin.

O Lord, have mercy upon us, have mercy upon us.

O Lord, let thy mercy be upon us, as our trust is in thee.

O Lord, in thee have I trusted; let me never be confounded.

LESSON FROM THE NEW TESTAMENT.

Let us pray.

O GOD, the Father of heaven, O God the Son, Redeemer of the world, O God the Holy Ghost, proceeding from the Father and the Son, O holy, blessed and glorious Trinity, three Persons and one God,
Have mercy upon us miserable sinners.

Remember not, Lord, our offences; neither take thou vengeance of our former sins; spare us, good Lord; spare thy people which thou hast redeemed with thy most precious blood, and be not angry with us forever;
Spare us, good Lord.

From all vain imaginations and delusions, from the sin that doth so easily beset us, from the temptations of the world, the flesh, and the devil, from all unhallowed and sinful affections, from all defilements of soul and spirit, from unbelief and contempt of thy word and commandments,
Good Lord, deliver us.

From all sedition, privy conspiracy and rebellion, from all heresy and schism, from a blinded conscience and from grieving thy Holy

---

NOTE.—This litany is from the work of Professor Hopkins, Auburn, N. Y. (altered).

Spirit, from an impenitent death, and from death everlasting,

Good Lord, deliver us.

From a wicked and hardened heart, from pride, covetousness and hypocrisy, from envy, hatred and all uncharitableness,

Good Lord, deliver us.

From sword, pestilence and famine, from lightning and tempest, from self-murder and sudden death, and from despair of thy mercy,

Good Lord, deliver us.

From all rash judging and evil speaking, from grudging at others' good, or repining at our own harm, from all murmuring at thy providences, and from a stubborn and rebellious mind,

Good Lord, deliver us.

By the mystery of thy spotless incarnation, by thy holy birth and baptism, by thy fasting and temptation in the wilderness, by thine agony and bloody sweat, by thy cross and passion, by thy precious death and burial, by thy glorious resurrection and ascension, by thy reigning at the right hand of God, and by the coming of the Holy Ghost the Comforter,

Good Lord, deliver us.

In all time of our tribulation, in all time of our extremity, in the hour of death, and in the day of judgment,

Good Lord, deliver us.

We sinners do beseech thee to hear us, O Lord,

and that thou wouldst grant us true repentance and amendment of life, that thou wouldst freely pardon all our sins and pour into all our hearts continually the grace of thy Holy Spirit,
We beseech thee to hear us, good Lord.

That thou wouldst give to us increase of faith, hope and charity, that thou wouldst grant unto all Christians the spirit of unity and peace, that thou wouldst heal our strifes and divisions, and shortly tread down Satan under our feet,
We beseech thee to hear us, good Lord.

That thou wouldst send forth laborers into thy harvest and be with thy servants who preach thy gospel among the nations, that thou wouldst disappoint the expectations of thine enemies and establish thy name in all the earth,
We beseech thee to hear us, good Lord.

That thou wouldst keep all thy servants, the ministers of thy gospel, in purity of doctrine and in holiness of life, that so holding fast the faithful word and walking as ensamples to the flock, they may both save themselves and those that hear them,
We beseech thee to hear us, good Lord.

That thou wouldst send down upon all Christian pastors and the congregations committed to their charge the healthful spirit of thy grace, that they may watch for souls as those that must give account, that thou wouldst revive true religion in the hearts of thy people, and that sinners may be converted unto thee,

We beseech thee to hear us, good Lord.

That thou wouldst bless all the rulers and judges of our land, giving them grace, that they bear not the sword in vain, but be a terror to evil-doers, and a praise to them that do well,

That thou wouldst bless and save our country, delivering us from all our iniquities and making us an ensample to the nations of peace and righteousness, that thou wouldst increase in us the power of true religion, and make us that happy people whose God is the Lord,

We beseech thee to hear us, good Lord.

That thou wouldst have compassion on all those that are drawn aside into lying idolatries and damnable heresies, even denying the Lord that bought them, that thou wouldst deliver thy people who are entangled in the snares of antichrist, and bring them to the knowledge and acknowledgment of the truth, those blind guides who lead the blind to destruction,

We beseech thee to hear us, good Lord.

That thou wouldst guard for us our land in peace, our atmosphere in purity, and wouldst give and preserve to us the kindly fruits of the earth, that in due season we may enjoy them,

We beseech thee to hear us, good Lord.

That thou wouldst have mercy upon all those who tempt thy people to sin, who follow in the steps of Balaam for a reward, and love the wages of unrighteousness,

That thou wouldst take pity on all that are oppressed and suffer wrong, that thou wouldst break the arm of the oppressor and speedily avenge thine elect who cry day and night unto thee without ceasing,

We beseech thee to hear us, good Lord.

Son of God, we beseech thee to hear us.

Son of God, we beseech thee to hear us.

O Lamb of God, who takest away the sins of the world,

Grant us thy peace.

And we humbly entreat thee, most merciful God, to receive graciously the sacrifices of praise and prayer which thy people have this day throughout the world offered unto thee.

Let the cry of thy family enter into thine ears, O Father, and send unto thy children an answer in peace through our Elder Brother Jesus Christ, who is also our high-Priest and Sacrifice.

Lord of all grace, purify, we beseech thee, our hearts by faith which is in Christ Jesus, and so cleanse us from all evil, that everything which beclouds and hinders the simple reception of thy truth may be put far from us, and the fruits of thy Spirit being made manifest in our lives and conversation, our eyes may be opened to behold wondrous things out of thy law, through Jesus Christ our Lord.

Special or extemporaneous Prayer.

HYMN.

SERMON.

Let us pray.

ALMIGHTY GOD, who hast given us grace at this time with one accord to make our common supplications unto thee, and dost promise that when two or three are gathered together in thy name thou wilt grant their requests; fulfil now, O Lord, the desires and petitions of thy servants, as may be most expedient for us, granting us in this world knowledge of thy truth, and in the world to come life everlasting. Amen.

HYMN AND DOXOLOGY.

BENEDICTION OR ASCRIPTION.

TENTH SUNDAY.

Afternoon or Evening Service.

There be many that say, Who will show us any good? Lord, lift thou up the light of thy countenance upon us.

Give ear to our words, O Lord; consider our meditation. Hearken unto the voice of our cry, our King, and our God; for unto thee will we pray.

Let us pray.

O LORD our God, look down on us and show us the riches of thy mercies and compassions; and so make us worthy, with a pure heart and a broken spirit, with hallowed lips and with a countenance that needeth not to be ashamed, to call upon thee; through Jesus Christ our Lord.

(*In unison.*)

Our Father, who art in heaven. hallowed be thy name, etc.

HYMN.

LESSON FROM THE OLD TESTAMENT.

SELECTION FROM THE PSALMS.

LESSON FROM THE NEW TESTAMENT.

Let us pray.

MOST merciful God, our heavenly Father, we bow with reverence and godly fear before thee. Thou art good; thy mercy endureth for ever; again hast thou opened thy hand to supply our wants, and caused all thy goodness to pass before us, and made the outgoings of the morning and evening to rejoice.

Blessed be thy name, O Lord.

But we confess that we are unthankful and evil; for we have not rendered unto thee according to the benefits received; we have not used our faculties and opportunities to thy glory, remembering that they are all thy gifts; neither have we glorified thee, our heavenly Master, with our bodies and our spirits, which are thine. We have indeed been unfaithful stewards of thy bounty and unprofitable servants. Pardon our iniquity, O Lord, for it is great.

Wherein this day we have not feared and loved thee, or have transgressed the law of charity, not loving our neighbor as ourselves; nor doing good as we have had opportunity; or have set our affections on things below, so that the love of the Father hath not been in us; or have indulged any sinful affection or unholy desire or passion; or have by our negligence and corruption grieved the Holy Spirit—be pleased, O Lord, of thy great mercy to forgive us our sins and purify us from all our defilements. And to this end, work in us a sincere repentance, and grant, that being redeemed from the power of sin, we may serve thee in newness of life and bring forth fruits worthy of repentance, to the glory of thy holy name.

O Lord, we pray thee come among us, and with great might succor us, that whereas, through our sin and wickedness, we are so much hindered in running the race that is set before us, thy bountiful grace and mercy may speedily help and deliver us, through Christ our Lord.

O God, thou fountain of all goodness, grant unto us a new heart and a right spirit, and according to thy promise put thy laws in our minds and write them upon our hearts, that we, knowing and constantly remembering thy will, may do at all times the things that please thee, and finally may be made partakers of thine eternal kingdom, through Jesus Christ our Lord.

O Lord, our merciful Father, who despiseth not the affliction of the afflicted, nor hideth thy face from such as are in any trouble or sorrow, hear thou those who call upon thee, and send them help and deliverance from thy holy habitation.

We pray for the coming of thy kingdom, O God. Let all the ends of the earth remember and turn unto the Lord; let all the kindreds of the nations worship before thee; for the kingdom is the Lord's, thou art the governor among the nations.

Let our kindred, our friends, and all whom thou hast made the instruments of thy goodness to us, share thy grace and mercy. Give unto them and us those things that are needful for the body, and with them bestow thy blessing and make us all to be partakers of thy grace and of the glory of our Lord Jesus Christ.

Bless those whom thou hast set over us; govern their hearts in thy fear, and guide their understandings to do those things which will be acceptable to thee and beneficial to us.

Comfort the comfortless and helpless; show the light of thy truth to those who wander out of the right way; give to all of us true repentance; strengthen and assist with thy grace those who have begun well, that they may persevere; keep us from all evil; and make us to continue in thy service to our lives' end, and then bring us to thine everlasting kingdom, through Jesus Christ our Lord.

On the earth and all that is therein, on the trade and merchandise of our people, on the labors by which men obtain thy abundant gifts,

We pray for thy blessing, O Lord.

On farmers and all tillers of the ground, on keepers of sheep and oxen, on all those by whose labors we are supplied with food,

We pray for thy blessing, O Lord.

On those who search for thy treasures hidden in the earth, on those who labor to make them fit for the use of man,
We pray for thy blessing, O Lord.

On those who labor in the building and adorning of the churches in which we worship and of the homes in which we live,
We pray for thy blessing, O Lord.

On manufacturers and handicraftsmen, on those who devise cunning works and are skilled in all manner of workmanship,
We pray for thy blessing, O Lord.

On merchants who bring thy gifts from foreign lands, on the men who go down to the sea in ships, and do business in great waters,
We pray for thy blessing, O Lord.

On all who trade with us in the shop, or in the market, on all who serve at the counter or in the office, on those who bring what we need for life, or comfort, or enjoyment, within reach of our homes,
We pray for thy blessing, O Lord.

On all who labor with the hands, on all who guide and govern their labors, on the employed and on the employer,
We pray for thy blessing, O Lord.

O Lord, who hast gone up on high to prepare a place for us in the mansions in thy Father's house; who hast promised that when thou comest thou wilt bring again those who sleep in thee; that when thou appearest we shall be like thee, for we shall see thee as thou art,

Have mercy upon us.

Grant us thy grace, that having this hope we may purify ourselves even as thou art pure, that whether we wake or sleep we may live with thee as thou hast died for us; that knowing thou wilt come at an hour when we think not, we may always watch and be ready; that our loins may be girded and our lights burning, and we ourselves like unto men that wait for their Lord; that when thou comest and knockest, whether in the second watch or in the third watch, we may open to thee immediately,

Grant us thy grace, O Lord.

That having the first fruits of the Spirit we may wait for the adoption, to wit, the redemption of our body,

Grant us thy grace, O Lord.

That our conversation being always in heaven, we may ever look for thee, our loving Saviour, to change our vile body and make it like unto thy glorious body,

Grant us thy grace, O Lord.

(*Special or extemporaneous Prayer.*)

HYMN.

SERMON.

Let us pray.

O GOD, who didst teach the hearts of thy faithful people by sending to them the light of thy Holy Spirit, grant us, by the same Spirit, a right understanding of thy saving truth. Visit, we pray thee, this congregation with thy love and favor; enlighten our minds more and more with the light of the everlasting gospel; graft in our hearts a love of the truth; increase in us true religion; nourish us with all goodness; and of thy great mercy keep us in the same, through Jesus Christ our Lord.

Lighten our darkness, we beseech thee, O Lord, and by thy great mercy defend us from all perils and dangers of this night, for the love of thine only Son, our Saviour Jesus Christ. Amen.

HYMN AND DOXOLOGY.

BENEDICTION OR ASCRIPTION.

AN ORDER OF BAPTISM FOR CHILDREN.

(The minister may commence the service with the following sentence:)

Our help is in the name of the Lord, who made heaven and earth.

(And he may then ask the parents:)

Do you offer this child to God and to his church, requiring that he shall be baptized?

(They shall answer:)

We do.

Let us pray.

Almighty God! who hast promised us, through thy goodness, to be our God, and the God of our children, as thou wast the God of Abraham and of his children; we pray thee to receive this child into the covenant of thy mercy, and to make *him* a partaker of thy grace; to the end that, when *he* shall have come to the age of discretion, *he* may adore and serve thee only, and may live and die in thee; so that the baptism through which we receive *him* into thy church may not have been administered to *him* in vain, but that he may be truly baptized into the death of thy Son, and into newness of life acceptable to thee; through Jesus Christ our Lord. Amen.

(*Then shall the minister say:*)

Hear ye the gospel which teacheth us the love of Christ, our Saviour, toward young children:

And they brought young children to him that he should touch them: and his disciples rebuked those that brought them. But when Jesus saw it he was much displeased, and said unto them, Suffer the little children to come unto me, and forbid them not, for of such is the kingdom of God. Verily, I say unto you, whosoever shall not receive the kingdom of God as a little child, he shall not enter therein. And he took them up in his arms, put his hands upon them, and blessed them.

(*The minister may then say to the parents:*)

You, who offer this child to be baptized, should consider that God must be served in spirit and in truth. You promise, before God and this assembly, that you will be careful, as far as by your duty you are bound and as necessity may require, to instruct this child in the Holy Scriptures and in the Christian faith which we confess in the Apostles' Creed. You will teach *him* to worship the only true God, to call upon him in all *his* necessities, to ascribe glory to him for all good, and to acknowledge that all *his* righteousness is in Christ Jesus, and all *his* strength in the sanctification of the Holy Spirit. You will teach *him* to deny himself, to take up *his* cross, and to keep the commandments of God, the substance of which is that we should love God with all our hearts, and our neighbor as ourselves. And you will take care to exhort this child, and to reprove *him* when it shall be necessary, so that *he* may be brought up in the fear of the Lord, and according to his holy word; to the end that *his* whole life may be employed for the glory of God, and for the edification of *his* neighbor. Do you promise this?

(*The parents shall answer:*)

We do.

(*The minister may then say:*)

The Lord give you grace faithfully to perform these promises.

(*The minister shall then baptize the child, naming him and saying:*)

I baptize thee in the name of the Father, and of the Son, and of the Holy Ghost. Amen.

(*After which the minister may use the following prayers:*)

O God! the Father, the Son, and the Holy Ghost! we beseech thee to accept and confirm in heaven what we have now done in thy name upon earth. Receive this child into the fold of the Good Shepherd, and bless *him* with all spiritual nurture.

O heavenly Father! who by the holy prophet

hast taught us that children are an heritage of the Lord; who also didst enjoin upon thy chosen people, Israel, to teach their children thy statutes and ordinances; and who, through thine apostle Peter, hast assured us that the promise is unto us and unto our children; we beseech thee to impress upon all parents and especially upon those who have at this time presented themselves before thee, a deep sense of the trust committed to them in thy wise providence. Sanctify them through thy truth; and give them opportunity and disposition to perform their duties in faithfulness and love. And give, O Father, to this child, and to all others who have been dedicated to thee in baptism, thy protecting care and grace. Give them meek and teachable dispositions and a continual growth in the knowledge of thy truth as they advance in years; to the end that, through the means of grace provided on earth, they may at last be received into the church of the first-born in heaven; through our Lord and Saviour Jesus Christ.

(Special or extemporaneous Prayer.)

The grace of our Lord Jesus Christ, and the love of God, and the communion of the Holy Ghost, be with us all, evermore. Amen.

AN ORDER OF BAPTISM FOR ADULTS.

(The minister may commence the service with the following sentence:)

Our help is in the name of the Lord, who made heaven and earth.

And then may ask the person to be baptized:)

Do you present yourself before God and his holy church for baptism?

(Answer:)

I do.

(Then the minister shall say:)

Hear, my brethren, how our Saviour instituted the holy sacrament of baptism, as it is recorded in the gospels:

And Jesus spake unto his disciples, saying, All power is given unto me in heaven and in earth. Go ye therefore, and teach all nations, baptizing them in the name of the Father, and of the Son, and of the Holy Ghost: teaching them to observe all things whatsoever I have commanded you.

And Jesus gave command to his disciples, saying, Go ye into all the world, and preach the gospel to every creature. He that believeth, and is baptized, shall be saved; but he that believeth not, shall be damned.

(*The minister shall then say to the person to be baptized:*)

Since our Lord hath instituted this holy sacrament of baptism, and hath commanded, as you have just heard, that it should be administered to all who believe in him; and since you have signified your desire to receive the same, in testimony of your faith, I proceed, in conformity with Holy Scripture, to administer it to you.

(*Then the minister shall offer the following prayer:*)

Almighty God, our heavenly Father, who hast promised us, through thy goodness, to be our God, and the God of all who believe in thee, and in Jesus Christ whom thou hast sent; we pray thee, to give thy Holy Spirit to thy servant who here presents *himself* in thy presence. Receive *him*, O God! into the covenant of thy mercy, and make *him* a partaker of thy grace; to the end that *he* may know thee as *his* God; that *he* may adore and serve thee only, and may live and die in thee: so that this baptism, through which we receive *him* into thy church, may not be administered to *him* in vain; but that *he* may be truly baptized into the death of thy Son, and into the newness of life acceptable unto thee; through Jesus Christ our Lord.   Amen.

(*The minister shall then say to the person to be baptized:*)

These are the holy engagements upon which you are about to enter through baptism:

In the presence of God and this assembly, you profess that you believe, and receive with all your heart, the Holy Scriptures; and that you desire to live and die in the Christian faith, which we confess in the Apostles' Creed. You profess to worship the only true God, and promise to call upon him in all your necessities, and to ascribe glory to him for all good. You profess to believe that all your righteousness is in Christ Jesus, and all your strength in the sanctification of the Holy Spirit. You promise, depending on divine aid, to renounce Satan and his works, the world with its vices, the flesh and its sinful desires; to deny yourself, to take up your cross, and to keep the commandments of God; the substance of which is, that we should love God with all our hearts, and our neighbor as ourselves. Finally, you promise to watch and pray, that you may live in the fear of God, and according to his holy word; to the end, that your whole life may be employed for the glory of God, and for the edification of your neighbor. Do you so profess and promise?

(*Answer:*)

I do.

(*The minister shall then baptize the person, naming him, and saying:*)

I baptize thee in the name of the Father, and of the Son, and of the Holy Ghost. Amen.

(*After which the minister may say to the baptized person:*)

You are now received into the number of the

faithful, and may be a partaker of the holy sacrament of the Supper.

May God give you grace to remember constantly the holy profession which you have made. May he accept and confirm in heaven that which we have done, in his name, and in his church on earth; and give you his blessing now and evermore. Amen.

(The minister shall then say:)

And I call upon you, Christian brethren, who are here present, to witness the profession which *this* person has made, in *his* baptism; and I exhort you to look upon *him* henceforth as a partaker with you of the same grace, and to offer up your prayers to God in *his* behalf.

Let us pray.

O gracious God! Father of mercy! we bless thee that thou hast been pleased to call us to a knowledge of thyself; and especially that thou hast given grace unto this person to enter into covenant with thee by baptism.

Grant, O merciful God! that *he* may constantly persevere in *his* holy profession. Since *he* has renounced Satan and his works, the world and its vices, the flesh and its sinful desires, let the prince of darkness have no power over *him;* and grant that, henceforth, *his* faith may triumph over the world, the flesh and its wicked propensities. Holy Father! sanctify *him* through thy truth; and make *him* fruitful in knowledge and in faith, in holiness and in comfort, all the days of *his* life; and, after having ministered in this world to the designs of thy providence, may *he* obtain from thy goodness eternal salvation; through Jesus Christ our Lord.

(*Special or extemporaneous Prayer.*)

The grace of our Lord Jesus Christ, and the love of God, and the communion of the Holy Ghost, be with us all evermore. Amen.

AN ORDER FOR RECEIVING MEMBERS INTO THE CHURCH.

The following-named persons having been duly and satisfactorily examined as to their faith in the Lord Jesus Christ, and their desire to be associated with this church, will rise in their places as their names are read. (*Read names*).

The following-named persons come to us on certificates from other churches. (*Read names*).

And they will all unite with us in this confession of our Common Faith.

(*The congregation rises and recites:*)

I believe in God the Father Almighty, Maker of heaven and earth:

And in Jesus Christ his only Son our Lord; who was conceived by the Holy Ghost, born of the Virgin Mary; suffered under Pontius Pilate, was crucified, dead, and buried; the third day he rose from the dead; he ascended into heaven, and sitteth on the right hand of God the Father Almighty; from thence he shall come to judge the quick and the dead.

I believe in the Holy Ghost; the holy Catholic Church—the communion of saints; the forgiveness of sins; the resurrection of the body; and the life everlasting. Amen.

Since our last communion the following have been dismissed to other churches. (*Read names*).

AN ORDER FOR THE ADMINISTRATION OF THE LORD'S SUPPER.

(Which may be used after any of the foregoing services, or as a distinct service. The minister may commence the service with the following:)

In the name of the Father, of the Son, and of the Holy Ghost.   Amen.

Let us pray.

O Eternal and Almighty God! whom we praise and glorify as our Creator and Sovereign Lord; we beseech thee, as we are now assembled to partake of the Holy Supper, which thy Son, our Saviour, Jesus Christ, commanded us to celebrate in remembrance of his death, that thou wouldst give us grace to perform this sacred duty, in a manner acceptable unto thee; through Jesus Christ our Lord.   Amen.

(The minister may then say:)

Hear, my brethren, the institution of the Lord's Supper, as it is related by St. Paul, in the eleventh chapter of the First Epistle to the Corinthians.

I have received of the Lord that which also I delivered unto you, that the Lord Jesus, the same night in which he was betrayed, took bread: and when he had given thanks, he brake it, and said, Take, eat; this is my body, which is broken for you: this do in remembrance of me. After the same manner also he took the cup, when he had supped, saying, This cup is the new testament in my blood: this do ye as oft as ye drink it, in remembrance of me. For as often as ye eat this bread, and drink this cup, ye do show the Lord's death till he come. Wherefore whosoever shall eat this bread, and drink this cup of the Lord, unworthily, shall be guilty of the body and blood of the Lord. But let a man examine himself, and so let him eat of that bread, and drink of that cup. For he that eateth and drinketh unworthily, eateth and drinketh condemnation to himself, not discerning the Lord's body.

You have now heard in what manner our Lord Jesus Christ instituted the Holy Supper; and with what purity and reverence it should be celebrated, even unto the end of the world, by all believers.

We learn from Holy Scripture, that none but true Christians should come thereunto, and that all such as are not of the number of the faithful are unworthy to be partakers thereof.

As for you, Christian brethren, who come to this holy communion, you ought carefully to consider what you are about to do, lest you eat of this bread and drink of this cup unworthily.

Judge ye yourselves, and ye shall not be judged of the Lord. And in all things, wherein ye know that ye have offended him, whether in word or in deed, in thought or in will, make confession thereof with a humble reliance upon his mercy, and a true desire to live, henceforth, a righteous and godly life. Be ye, also, filled with sincere love toward your neighbor; if ye have done wrong to any, make reparation; and forgive ye one another, even as ye desire from God the forgiveness of your sins. If ye are thus minded, and if your consciences thus bear witness for you before God, who knoweth your hearts, ye may come to this holy table; and ye ought not to doubt that the Lord Jesus will there make you partakers of all the fruits of his passion and death.

But let us give our humble and hearty thanks to God, for the redemption of the world through Jesus Christ his Son; who did humble himself even to the death of the cross, for us miserable sinners, that he might make us children of God, and exalt us to everlasting life; and, to the end that we should always remember his exceeding great love, did institute this holy sacrament, to be unto us a pledge of his love, and a perpetual memorial of his death, to our great comfort. To this merciful Redeemer, therefore, as well as to the Father and the Holy Spirit, let us now and always offer, as we are most bounden, our prayers and praises.

Let us pray.

It is meet and right, and our profitable duty, that we should, at all times and in all places, give thanks unto thee, O Lord, Holy Father, Everlasting God! through Jesus Christ our Lord; who for us was made very man, yet without sin; who died for our offences, and rose again for our justification; who by his death hath destroyed death, and by his resurrection hath given us eternal life; who hath ascended up on high, far above all heavens, where he ever liveth to make intercession for us; who also, according to his gracious promise, sent down upon the Apostles the Holy Spirit, to lead them into all truth, and to bestow upon them the gift of tongues, that they might preach the gospel unto all nations; whereby we have been brought out of darkness into light, and to a knowledge of thee; who also giveth us the Spirit of Adoption, and the blessed hope of pardon and peace, at the day of his glorious appearing.

(*The following may be sung by the choir or congregation, or read by the minister:*)

Therefore, with angels and archangels, and with all the company of heaven, we laud and magnify thy glorious name; evermore praising thee, and saying, Holy, holy, holy, Lord God of Hosts, heaven and earth are full of thy glory, Glory be to thee, O Lord, most high!

And since, O Father, Jesus Christ, thy Son, did offer himself as a sacrifice on the Cross, to redeem mankind, we beseech thee, in consideration of this sacrifice, that thou wouldst receive the supplications which we offer unto thy Divine Majesty, for the peace of the whole world, and for the salvation of all people.

We pray thee to bless the Church Universal, with the spirit of truth, unity and concord; and to give grace to all who profess thy name, to follow with one consent thy holy word, and live in harmony and godly love.

And grant, O God! who art the source of all power, thy grace, to bless and defend all Christian rulers and magistrates, especially the President of the United States. So replenish them with the grace of thy Holy Spirit, that they may perform their duties with faithfulness, that religion may flourish, and righteousness advance among us.

Shed thy grace, O Shepherd of our souls! upon all the ministers of thy church, that they may set forth the truth and power of thy holy word, both by their life and doctrine; that they may faithfully administer thy holy sacraments, and diligently watch over the flocks committed to their charge.

We beseech thee, of thy goodness, to succor all persons who, during this transitory life, are in trouble, sorrow, need, sickness, or any other adversity.

And, O Lord! we pray for all this congregation, for all thy servants who desire to be partakers at thy table, and for all who show forth the death of their Saviour, and wait for his glorious coming; that through the communion in the death of thy

Son, and through the efficacy of the precious blood which he shed upon the cross, we may be delivered from the wrath to come, and be found worthy to be received, with all thine elect, into the glory of thy kingdom.

Hear us, O God, our Father! in the name of Jesus Christ, our Saviour and Intercessor, who hath taught us thus to pray:

Our Father which art in heaven, hallowed be thy name, etc.

Almighty God! Father of our Lord Jesus Christ, before whom we now come to partake of the sacrament of the death of thy Son, graciously hear the confession of our sins. We acknowledge, O Lord, our unworthiness; we deplore the enormity and number of the sins which we have committed against thee; and we do not presume to come to thy holy sacrament, trusting in our own righteousness, but in thy great compassion. Have mercy upon us, O merciful Father! have mercy upon us. Pardon us, for the love of Jesus Christ; and give us grace this day, so to receive these sacred mysteries of bread and wine, that being united to thy holy Son through faith, we may live in him and he in us. We beseech thee to hear us, for the sake of the same Jesus Christ, our Lord. Amen.

(*The minister may then give the following invitation:*)

You who are sensible of your lost and helpless

state by sin; who depend upon the atonement of Christ for acceptance with God; who are in sincere charity with all your neighbors; and are resolved to conform your lives more and more to the commandments of God, are cordially invited to partake of the holy communion of the body and blood of our Lord.

Let us pray.

O Lord, we thank thee for the ordinances of thine house, and for the institution of the Lord's Supper. Help us to enter into its divine purpose, and to understand its spiritual meaning.

We desire to be one with the Saviour. Feed us with the bread which came down from heaven. Pour the spirit of Christ's life into our souls. Strengthen our minds and hearts by the truth. Cleanse our consciences from guilt and sin by the blood of Jesus. May we eat and drink at thy table, as thy children, in fellowship with our elder brother, who has prepared for us this feast of redemption. May no entertainment be so grateful, no communion so sweet, as the Supper of the Lord, the intercourse with our glorified Redeemer through the breaking of bread, and the participation of the cup offered to us this day.

We desire, also, to be one with Christ's Church: to be members of that mystical body, of which he is the head, and which he fills with a life like his own. May we cherish the love which suffereth long and is kind; which beareth all things; believeth all things; hopeth all things; endureth all things. Assist us, O Lord, to understand this inspired lesson, so closely connected with the fellowship of Christianity, in which we this day engage. May we be animated and guided by the example of our blessed Lord in our endeavors to cultivate this charity. His love constrains us not to live to ourselves. Dispose us, we beseech thee, to strive after a life of pure and noble self-sacrifice in his blessed service.

Bless our fellow-communicants. May they be refreshed by the spiritual manifestation of Christ to their souls; and may they sit down with us together in the kingdom of God when time shall be no more.

Now, O Divine Redeemer, who art the bread of life broken for us, look upon us, thy disciples, as we are gathered at this table. For it is thy table, and we are thy guests, though we are not worthy to eat the crumbs that fall from it. We know that thou art here, though we cannot see thee nor hear thy voice. Thou seest us—thou knowest us all by name. Make thyself known to us in the breaking of the bread, and help us to discern the Lord's body. We would thank thee for the bread—we bless thee for it. We pray that our souls may feed upon it, and that we may be made strong in our faith.

(Special prayers.)

We ask all for thine own name's sake. Amen.

(*Here the bread is given to the elders who offer it to the communicants. Then the minister may say:*)

After the Supper our Lord took the cup and gave thanks to God his Father.

Let us also give thanks to God for his great mercies.

We give thanks to thee, O Lord God, Father of our Lord Jesus Christ, for thy great mercy in permitting us to sit together in these heavenly places in Christ Jesus. We do thank thee for his life and death, for his resurrection and ascension, and that he now sitteth at thy right hand in glory everlasting.

(*Special thanksgiving.*)

Now we bless thee for the cup which is to be given to us. And we pray thee bless the cup to us. As we receive it give us faith to believe that Christ died for our sins, that he shed his blood for us, and that his blood cleanseth from all sins. Cleanse our hearts, O Divine Redeemer, from all our sins and from this time make us new creatures, so that we may live as those ought to live who have been bought with the precious blood of the Son of God. Make this cup to be life indeed to all who partake of it. Amen.

(*Then the minister may say:*)

This cup, saith our Lord, is the new covenant in my blood. Drink ye all of it, for as oft as ye eat this bread and drink this cup, ye do show the Lord's death till he come.

(*Here the cup is given to the elders who offer it to the communicants. After which may be said or sung the following:*)

Glory be to God on high,
And on earth peace, good-will toward men.
We praise thee, we bless thee, we worship thee,
We glorify thee, we give thanks to thee for thy great glory.
O Lord God, heavenly King,
God the Father Almighty.
O Lord, the only begotten Son, Jesus Christ,
O Lord God, Lamb of God, Son of the Father,
That takest away the sins of the world,
Have mercy upon us:
Thou that takest away the sins of the world,
Receive our prayer:
Thou that sittest at the right hand of God the Father,
Have mercy upon us:
For thou only art holy,
Thou only art the Lord;
Thou only, O Christ, with the Holy Ghost,
Art most high in the glory of God the Father.
Amen.

(*The exhortation to those who have communed:*)

I now exhort and beseech you, my brethren, by the mercies of God, and by the love of the Lord

Jesus, to consider well what we have just done, in the holy rite which we have celebrated.

We have solemnly acknowledged, by this act of thanksgiving, and by this public profession of our faith, that we have been ransomed from our sins and from condemnation, by the death of Jesus Christ. We have testified that we are all brethren and members of one body, and that we have a brotherly and sincere love towards each other. We have also promised to glorify God in our minds and bodies, by a life of holiness, worthy of our vocation.

May God give us grace to remember well these promises, to perform them religiously, and to have the death of our beloved Redeemer so deeply graven in our hearts, that we may die daily, more and more, unto sin, and that we may walk in the ways of holiness all our lives, to the glory of God, and to our mutual edification.

(*The service may be concluded with one of the following benedictions:*)

Now the God of peace, that brought again from the dead our Lord Jesus, that great Shepherd of the sheep, through the blood of the everlasting covenant, make you perfect in every good work to do his will, working in you that which is well pleasing in his sight, through Jesus Christ; to whom be glory forever and ever. Amen.

The Lord bless you and keep you. The Lord

make his face to shine upon you, and be gracious unto you. The Lord lift up his countenance upon you, and give you peace. Amen.

The grace of our Lord Jesus Christ, and the love of God, and the communion of the Holy Ghost, be with us all evermore. Amen.

AN ORDER FOR THE ADMINISTRATION OF THE LORD'S SUPPER, IN THE CHAMBER OF THE SICK.

As we are now about to celebrate the Holy Communion of the body and blood of Christ, let us consider how St. Paul exhorteth all persons to examine themselves before they eat of that bread, and drink of that cup. For the benefit is great, if with a truly penitent heart and lively faith we receive this holy sacrament—for then we spiritually eat the flesh of Christ, and drink his blood; then we dwell in Christ and Christ in us, we are one with Christ and Christ with us.

Let us examine ourselves, therefore, to know whether we truly repent of our sins, and whether, trusting in God's mercy, we will seek our whole salvation in Jesus Christ.

If we have this testimony in our hearts before God, our sins are forgiven through the perfect merits of Jesus Christ our Lord; and we may come to his holy table.

And although we have not perfect faith, and do not serve God with such zeal as we ought, but have daily to fight against the lusts of our flesh; yet if, by God's grace, we are heartily sorry for these weaknesses, and earnestly desire to withstand all unbelief, and to keep all his commandments, we may be sure our remaining sins and infirmities do not prevent us from being received of God in mercy, and so made worthy partakers of this heavenly food.

For we come not to this Supper as righteous in ourselves, but we come to seek our life in Christ. Let us, then, look upon this sacrament as a comfort for those who are sick, and consider that the worthiness our Lord requireth of us is, that we be truly sorry for our sins, and find our joy and salvation in him. United with him who is holy, even our Lord Jesus Christ, we are accepted of the Father, and invited to partake of these holy things which are for holy persons.

Let us attend to the words of the institution of the Holy Supper of our Lord Jesus Christ, as they are delivered by the Apostle Paul: "I have received of the Lord that which also I delivered unto you, that the Lord Jesus, the same night in which he was betrayed, took bread: and when he had given thanks, he brake it, and said, Take, eat; this is my body, which is broken for you: this do in remembrance of me. After the same manner also he took the cup, when he had supped, saying, This cup is the new testament in my blood: this do ye as oft as ye drink it, in remembrance of me. For as often as ye eat this bread, and drink this cup, ye do show the Lord's death till he come."

And now, that we may fulfil the Saviour's institution with righteousness and joy, let us, in celebrating this sacred service, follow his holy example in word and action.

As the Lord Jesus, the night in which he was betrayed, took bread, we take these elements to be set apart to the holy use and mystery for which he has appointed them, and as he gave thanks and blessed, let us now draw near to the throne of grace, and present to God our

Prayers and thanksgivings.

Almighty and eternal God, with thy holy church throughout all the world we believe in thee the Father Almighty, Maker of heaven and earth; and in Jesus Christ thine only Son our Lord, who was conceived by the Holy Ghost, born of the Virgin Mary, suffered under Pontius Pilate, was crucified, dead, and buried: the third day he rose again from the dead; he ascended into heaven, and sitteth on the right hand of God the Father Almighty; from thence he shall come to judge the quick and the dead. We believe in the Holy Ghost; the holy catholic church, the communion of saints; the forgiveness of sins; the resurrection of the body; and the life everlasting.

Almighty God, our heavenly Father, who admittest thy people into such wonderful communion, that partaking of the body and blood of thy dear Son, they should dwell in him, and he in them; we unworthy sinners, approaching thy presence, and beholding thy glory, do abhor ourselves, and repent in dust and ashes. We have grievously sinned against thee in thought, in word, and in deed, provoking most justly thy wrath and indignation against us. We have broken our vows, we have dishonored thy holy name, and are unworthy of the least of all thy mercies.

We confess that we are not worthy that thou shouldst come under our roof; and that we deserve not to eat of the crumbs which fall from thy table.

Yet now, most gracious Father, have mercy upon us; for the sake of Jesus Christ forgive us all our sins; purify us from all uncleanness in spirit and in flesh: enable us heartily to forgive others as we beseech thee to forgive us; and grant that we may hereafter serve thee in newness of life to the glory of thy holy name.

And we most humbly beseech thee, O merciful Father, to vouchsafe unto us thy gracious presence, as we now make that memorial of his most blessed sacrifice which thy Son hath commanded us to make: and to bless and sanctify with thy Word and Spirit these thine own gifts of bread and wine which we set before thee; that we, receiving them, according to our Saviour's institution, in thankful remembrance of his death and passion, may, through the power of the Holy Ghost, be made partakers of his body and blood, with all his benefits, to our salvation and the glory of thy most holy name. Amen.

Our Father who art in heaven, hallowed be thy name, etc.

According to the holy institution, example, and command of our Lord Jesus Christ, and in remembrance of him, we do this: who the same night in which he was betrayed, took bread:

(Here the minister shall take some of the bread into his hands.)

And when he had given thanks, he brake it,

(Here he shall break the bread.)

And said, Take, eat; this is my body which is broken for you: this do in remembrance of me.

(Here the bread is given.)

After the same manner also he took the cup,

(Here he shall take the cup into his hand.)

When he had supped, saying, This cup is the new testament in my blood: this do ye, as oft as ye drink it, in remembrance of me.

(Here the cup is to be given.)

The peace of the Lord Jesus Christ be with us.

Since the Lord hath now fed our souls at his table, let us praise his holy name with thanksgiving, who hath not spared his own Son, but delivered him for us all, and given us all things with him; who commendeth his love toward us, in that, while we were yet sinners, Christ died for us; much more then, being now justified by his blood, we shall be saved from wrath through him. For if, when we were enemies, we were reconciled to God by the death of his Son; much more, being reconciled, we shall be saved by his life. Let us, therefore, show forth his praise from this time by glorifying God in our bodies and in our spirits, which are his; ever walking worthy of his grace, and of our high calling in Christ Jesus.

Let us pray.

Almighty and everlasting God, we most heartily thank thee that thou hast now fed us with the spiritual food of the most precious body and blood of thy Son, our Saviour Jesus Christ; assuring us thereby that we are heirs through hope, of thine everlasting kingdom.

And here we offer and present ourselves, our souls and bodies, to be a holy and living sacrifice unto thee, which is our reasonable service; beseeching thee that we who have partaken of this sacrament may continue in the holy fellowship and communion of thy saints; in faith, charity, patience, and all the fruits of the Spirit; and may constantly do all such good works as thou hast prepared for us to walk in.

Comfort and succor, we beseech thee, all thy people who are in trouble, sorrow, need, sickness, or any other adversity.

Especially we commend unto thee those departing this life: be present to them, in thy mercy and thy love, in that last hour when heart and flesh do fail; defend them against the assaults of the devil, and give them such patient hope and confidence that they may joyfully commit their spirits to thy hands, and do thou receive them to thy rest.

The grace of the Lord Jesus Christ, and the love of God, and the communion of the Holy Spirit, be with us all.   Amen.

AN ORDER FOR THE CEREMONY OF MARRIAGE.

(The minister may commence the service with the following sentence:)

Our help is in the name of the Lord, who made heaven and earth.

(Then the minister may say:)

God our Father, having created heaven and earth, and all that in them is, made man in his own image, and gave him dominion over the beasts of the field, over the fish of the sea, over the fowl of the air, and over every living thing that moveth upon the earth. And after he had created man, God said, It is not good that the man should be alone: I will make him an helpmeet for him. And the Lord God made woman, bone of his bone, and flesh of his flesh, signifying thereby that they two were one.

Wherefore, our blessed Lord, when the Pharisees came unto him, tempting him, and saying unto him, Is it lawful for a man to put away his wife for every cause? answered and said unto them: Have ye not read, that he which made them at the beginning, made them male and female, and said, For this cause shall a man leave father and mother, and shall cleave to his wife; and they twain shall be one flesh? So then they are no more twain, but one flesh.

What, therefore, God hath joined together, let no man put asunder.

And the Apostle Paul, who commendeth marriage as honorable in all, saith: So ought men to love their wives as their own bodies; he that loveth his wife, loveth himself. For no man ever yet hated his own flesh, but nourisheth and cherisheth it. Likewise, let the wife see that she reverence her husband, as it is fit in the Lord.

Seeing, then, that this holy covenant of matrimony, which God hath ordained, is of such authority and obligation, it is not to be entered into unadvisedly or lightly; but reverently, discreetly and soberly, in the fear of God, and with holy purpose to live therein in all purity, according to his will.

(Addressing the persons to be married, the minister may say:)

Are you willing to enter into the holy state of matrimony, which God hath instituted, to live together therein, according to his commandments?

(They shall answer:)

We are.

And do you desire to make known here, before God and this company, this your purpose?

(They shall answer:)

We do.

(Then the minister may say:)

God confirm and bless your purpose.

Let us pray.

O eternal God! the author of every good and perfect gift, we thank thee that thou hast ordained the institution of marriage; and we beseech thee to send thy blessing upon these thy servants, who are now about to be joined together in this holy estate. Give them a just sense of thy presence, and of the obligation of the covenant they are about to make; to the end that this solemn service may have a wholesome influence upon their affections and conduct throughout life, to the glory of thy name, through Jesus Christ our Lord. Amen.

(*The minister may then say to the man:*)

―――, Do you acknowledge here, before God and this company, that you have agreed to take, and that you now take, ――― for your wife? Do you promise to love, honor and protect her; to maintain, comfort and cherish her, in health and in sickness, in joy and in sorrow, in prosperity and in adversity; to lead a holy life with her, being faithful unto her in all things until death do you part, as is the duty of a good husband, according to the word of God?

Answer.—I do.

(*The minister may then say to the woman:*)

―――, Do you also acknowledge here, before God and this company, that you have agreed to take, and that you now take, ――― for your husband? Do you promise to love and honor him; to comfort and cherish him, in health and in sickness, in joy and in sorrow, in prosperity and in adversity; to lead a holy life with him, being faithful unto him in all things until death do you part, as is the duty of a good wife, according to the word of God?

Answer.—I do.

(*To be used or not, at the discretion of the parties.*)

In testimony that you, ——— and ———, do advisedly and solemnly ratify all that hath been declared and promised by you, do thou, ———, acknowledge and endow this woman as thy wife, by delivering unto her a ring, in token of thy faith; and do thou, ———, in like manner receive the same, as a pledge of his faith, and as a witness of thy vows?

(*Then the man delivers to the woman a ring, placing it upon the fourth finger of her left hand. Then shall the minister join their right hands together and say:*)

You are now husband and wife.

Those whom God hath joined together, let not man put asunder.

Let us pray to God our Father for his blessing upon these his servants.

O Almighty, all-merciful, and all-wise God! we beseech thee, in behalf of these persons, who have entered into the holy estate of marriage, that thou wouldst vouchsafe to them thy Holy Spirit. Send down thy blessing upon these thy servants, whom we bless in thy name. Enable them to observe surely, and to perform faithfully, the vows and covenant between them made; and, mutually edifying each other, to live together in purity, concord and piety. Give them grace to reverence and serve thee, and to contribute to the advancement of thy glory, the honor of the gospel and the welfare of thy church. Favorably hear us, O Father of Mercy! in the name and for the sake of thy dear Son. Amen.

(Special prayers.)
(Then the minister may add this benediction:)

God, the Father, the Son and God the Holy Ghost, bless, preserve and guide you. May you be filled with all spiritual benediction, and so live together in this life that, in the world to come, you may have life everlasting. Amen.

AN ORDER FOR THE BURIAL SERVICE FOR A CHILD.

AND the Lord struck the child, ... and it was very sick. David therefore besought God for the child; and David fasted, and went in and lay all night upon the earth. And the elders of his house arose, and went to him to raise him up from the earth: but he would not, neither did he eat bread with them. And it came to pass, on the seventh day, that the child died. And the servants of David feared to tell him that the child was dead; for they said, Behold, while the child was yet alive, we spake unto him, and he would not hearken unto our voice; how will he then vex himself, if we tell him that the child is dead? But when David saw that his servants whispered, David perceived that the child was dead; therefore David said unto his servants, Is the child dead? And they said, He is dead. Then David arose from the earth, and washed, and anointed himself, and changed his apparel, and came into the house of the Lord, and worshipped; then he came to his own house; and when he required, they set bread before him, and he did eat. Then said his servants unto him, What thing is this that thou hast done? Thou didst fast and weep for the child, while it was alive; but when the child was dead, thou didst rise and eat bread. And he said, While the child was yet alive, I fasted and wept; for I said, who can tell whether God will be gracious to me, that the child may live? But now he is dead, wherefore should I fast? can I bring him back again? I shall go to him, but he shall not return to me. . . . .

Jesus said, Suffer little children, and forbid them not, to come unto me: for of such is the kingdom of heaven. It is not the will of your Father which is in heaven that one of these little ones should perish. For I say unto you, That in heaven their angels do always behold the face of my Father which is in heaven. . . . .

O Lord, our Lord, how excellent is thy name in all the earth! Out of the mouth of babes and sucklings thou hast perfected praise. . . . . I thank thee, O Father, Lord of heaven and earth, because thou hast hid these things from the wise and prudent, and hast revealed them unto babes; even so, Father, for so it seemed good in thy sight. . . . .

We have not an High Priest which cannot be touched with the feeling of our infirmities; but was in all points tempted like as we are, yet without sin. Let us, therefore, come boldly unto the throne of grace, that we may obtain mercy, and find grace to help in time of need. . . . .

The Lord gave, and the Lord hath taken away; blessed be the name of the Lord. . . . .

(*Here the address may be made.*)

Let us pray.

(*Any of these prayers may be used.*)

Eternal and ever-blessed God, out of the depths of our sin and sorrow, we, the frail children of the dust, would lift up our souls unto thee.

Through all time and change thou art the same: irresistible in might, yet infinite in wisdom, love and mercy; our refuge and our strength; our hope, and help and comfort; our God and Father in Christ.

Clouds and darkness are round about thee, but justice and judgment are the habitation of thy throne; mercy and truth go before thy face. Though thou slay us, yet will we trust in thee. Our flesh and our heart fail, but thou art the strength of our heart and our portion forever.

Blessed be thy name, O God, that in thine unspeakable love thou didst send thy well-beloved Son into this world to be our Saviour, that even as sin had reigned unto death, so grace might reign through righteousness unto eternal life, by Jesus Christ our Lord.

Father of mercies and God of all comfort, who dost not afflict willingly the children of men, but lovest those whom thou chastenest, draw near, we earnestly beseech thee, with thine own abundant consolations, to us who are sorrowing for the dead, so that while we mourn, we may not murmur nor faint under thy rod; but, remembering thine unnumbered past and present mercies, thy promises and all thy love in Christ, may resign ourselves meekly into thy hands, to be taught and disciplined by thee. Thou, Lord, knowest our condition, our sorrows and the secrets of our hearts. Pour into our wounded spirits the balm of thy fatherly wisdom and compassion; and grant that, loosened from earthly ties, we may cleave the more closely to thee, who bringest life out of death, and who canst turn our grief into eternal joy.

And now, O merciful God, vouchsafe unto us, who are still spared, grace to receive aright the warnings of thy providence and the lessons taught us by the life and death of our fellowmen. May every instance of mortality convince us of the evil of sin and the vanity of earthly things, and lead us unto him in whom pardon, peace and life are to be found, so that we may be delivered from both the power of sin and the fear of death. And grant that, whensoever our call shall come, our souls may depart in peace and our bodies rest in hope to rise in glory, through the might and merits of Jesus Christ our Saviour; for whom, and through whom, we desire, in life and in death, to bless thy name; and to whom, with thee and the Holy Ghost, we would ascribe all glory and praise, world without end. Amen.

O merciful God, Father of our Lord Jesus Christ, who hath said, Blessed are they that

mourn, for they shall be comforted: under the shadow of thy judgment we come to thee, and acknowledge thee to be the Lord alone. Thou hast entered this house with thy chastenings. O be thou nigh in thy tender compassion to these afflicted ones. Bless thy sorrowing servants with thine abounding consolations. Convert them wholly to thyself, and fill their bleeding hearts with thy love. Make the night of their grief to be light by thy grace. Deliver us, thy servants, we pray thee, from the bondage of our sins, that we may be free from fear of death and may be ready at thy coming. Yea, Lord, for Christ's sake, sanctify us by thy Holy Spirit, that whether we live, we may live unto the Lord, or whether we die, we may die unto the Lord; whether we live or die, may we be the Lord's.
Amen.

O God, whose days are without end and whose mercies cannot be numbered, make us, we beseech thee, deeply sensible of the shortness and uncertainty of human life, and let thy Holy Spirit lead us through this vale of misery, in holiness and righteousness, all the days of our lives; that when we shall have served thee in our generation, we may be gathered unto our fathers, having the testimony of a good conscience; in the communion of thy Church; in the confidence of a certain faith; in the comfort of a reasonable, religious and holy hope; in favor with thee, our God, and in perfect charity with the world; all which we ask through Jesus Christ our Lord. Amen.

(Special prayers.)

Our Father which art in heaven, hallowed be thy name, etc.

Now the God of peace, that brought again from the dead our Lord Jesus Christ, that great Shepherd of the sheep, through the blood of the everlasting covenant, make you perfect in every good work to do his will, working in you that which is well-pleasing in his sight, through Jesus Christ; to whom be glory forever and ever. Amen.

(If it be desired, the following service may be used at the grave:)

(When the body has been lowered into the grave, the minister may say:)

Let us pray.

O merciful God, the Father of our Lord Jesus Christ, who is the Resurrection and the Life; in whom whosoever believeth shall live, though he die; and whosoever liveth and believeth in him shall not die eternally; who also hath taught us, by his holy apostle St. Paul, not to be sorry, as men without hope, for them that sleep in him; we meekly beseech thee, O Father, to raise us from the death of sin unto the life of righteousness, that, when we shall depart this life, we may rest in him; and that, at the general resurrection in the last day, we may be found acceptable in thy sight and receive that blessing which thy well-beloved Son shall then pronounce to all that love and fear thee, saying, Come, ye blessed of my Father, receive the kingdom prepared for you from the foundation of the world; Grant this, we beseech thee, O merciful Father, through Jesus Christ, our Mediator and Redeemer. Amen.

The grace of the Lord Jesus Christ, and the love of God and the communion of the Holy Ghost, be with us all. Amen.

AN ORDER FOR THE BURIAL SERVICE FOR AN ADULT.

(The minister may recite the following introductory sentences:)

Man that is born of a woman is of few days, and full of trouble. He cometh forth like a flower, and is cut down: he fleeth also as a shadow, and continueth not.

Man dieth and wasteth away: yea, man giveth up the ghost, and where is he?

I am the Resurrection and the Life, saith the Lord; he that believeth in me, though he were dead, yet shall he live: and whosoever liveth and believeth in me shall never die.

(Then may be said or sung this Psalm:)

Lord, thou hast been our dwelling-place in all generations.

Before the mountains were brought forth, or ever thou hadst formed the earth and the world, even from everlasting to everlasting thou art God.

Thou turnest man to destruction; and sayest, Return, ye children of men.

For a thousand years in thy sight are but as yesterday when it is past, and as a watch in the night.

Thou carriest them away as with a flood; they are as a sleep: in the morning they are like grass which groweth up.

In the morning it flourisheth and groweth up; in the evening it is cut down and withereth.

The days of our years are threescore years and ten; and if by reason of strength they be fourscore years, yet is their strength labor and sorrow, for it is soon cut off, and we fly away.

So teach us to number our days, that we may apply our hearts unto wisdom.

(Or this:)

Lord, make me to know mine end, and the measure of my days, what it is; that I may know how frail I am.

Behold, thou hast made my days as an handbreadth, and mine age is as nothing before thee; verily every man at his best state is altogether vanity.

Surely every man walketh in a vain show; surely they are disquieted in vain; he heapeth up riches, and knoweth not who shall gather them.

And now, Lord, what wait I for? my hope is in thee.

Deliver me from all my transgressions; and make me not the reproach of the foolish.

I was dumb, I opened not my mouth; because thou didst it.

When thou with rebukes dost correct man for iniquity, thou makest his beauty to consume away like a moth; surely every man is vanity.

Hear my prayer, O Lord, and give ear unto my

cry; hold not thy peace at my tears; for I am a stranger with thee, and a sojourner, as all my fathers were.

(After which may follow this lesson:)

But I would not have you to be ignorant, brethren, concerning them which are asleep, that ye sorrow not, even as others which have no hope. For if we believe that Jesus died and rose again, even so them also which sleep in Jesus will God bring with him. For this we say unto you, by the word of the Lord, that we which are alive and remain until the coming of the Lord, shall not prevent them which are asleep. For the Lord himself shall descend from heaven with a shout, with the voice of the archangel, and with the trump of God; and the dead in Christ shall rise first. Then we, which are alive and remain, shall be caught up together with them in the clouds, to meet the Lord in the air; and so shall we ever be with the Lord. Wherefore comfort one another with these words.

(Then may follow any of these or other prayers.)

Let us pray.

We humble ourselves, O Lord God, before thy Divine Majesty, acknowledging that we are guilty in thy sight; for we have sinned and done wickedly; and the wages of sin is death.

But we thank and praise thee, that of thine

unspeakable compassion and grace, thou hast sent thy well-beloved Son into the world, to redeem and deliver us, that we, who by our sins lay in death, might be made heirs, according to the hope of everlasting life; that as sin hath reigned unto death, so might grace reign through righteousness unto eternal life, by Jesus Christ our Lord.

Almighty and everlasting God, who sendest forth thy Spirit and we are created, and who takest away our breath and we die and return to the dust, we bow in reverence before thine inscrutable providence; remembering that thou, who orderest all things according to thine own will in heaven and earth, art also our merciful and loving Father, who dost not willingly afflict or grieve the children of men, but dost correct us, that we may be partakers of thy holiness. We would therefore be subject unto thee, saying, The Lord gave, and the Lord hath taken away; blessed be the name of the Lord. Amen.

(*Here an address may be made.*)

Let us pray.

And now we follow to the house appointed for all living, the dust of our dear *brother*, whom thou hast been pleased to call out of this sinful and dying world; to commit *his* body to the grave; till that great day when earth and sea shall give up their dead:

Not sorrowing as others who have no hope; but believing, that as Jesus died and rose again, so also them that sleep in Jesus thou wilt bring with him; that being cleansed from sin, and redeemed from the bondage of death, they may reign in immortal life, with Christ our Lord, who shall change our vile body, that it may be fashioned like unto his glorious body, according to that working whereby he is able to subdue all things unto himself.

I heard a voice from heaven, saying unto me, Write, Blessed are the dead that die in the Lord from henceforth; yea, saith the Spirit, that they may rest from their labors, and their works do follow them.

Lord, increase our faith.

Merciful God, Father of our Lord Jesus Christ, we give thee humble and hearty thanks for all thy servants who are fallen asleep in the Lord, and have received the end of their faith, even the salvation of their souls.

For all thy goodness and mercy vouchsafed to them in their earthly pilgrimage, we give thee praise and glory.

It is of thy grace that they fought the good fight and kept the faith, and have obtained the unfading crown, being conquerors, yea, more than conquerors, through him that loved us.

We magnify thy name, O God, our Father and their Father, that, their trials and temptations being ended, sickness and death being passeb, with all the dangers and miseries of this present life, they have entered into the joy of their Lord, and are in perfect peace and felicity in thy presence forever; their spirits being with thee, and their bodies resting in the grave until the resurrection of the just.

May we, animated by their good examples, run the race that is set before us; not being weary in well-doing, or fainting when we are rebuked of thee; that, when this transitory world is passed away, we may again be joined with our dear friends, departed in the Lord, in a perfect union and communion forever, in thy kingdom of glory, where there shall be no more sickness or sighing, pain, sorrow, or death, for the former things shall have passed away.

Grant us true repentance, and remission of all our sins; cleanse us from all our iniquities; deliver us from the dominion of sin, that we may be delivered from the fear and the power of death. And not knowing at what hour the Lord shall come, may we be sober and watch unto prayer, daily meditating on mortality, and immortality, and giving all diligence to make our calling and election sure; that when Christ, who is our life, shall appear, we may appear with him, and receive that sentence, Come, ye blessed of my Father, inherit the kingdom prepared for you from the foundation of the world.

Special Prayers.

These things we ask, not in our own name, or trusting in our own worthiness, but for thy mercy's sake, through our Lord and Saviour Jesus Christ, who died for our sins, and rose again for our justification, and who taught us thus to pray:

Our Father, who art in heaven, hallowed be thy name, etc.

BENEDICTION.

The grace of our Lord Jesus Christ, and the love of God, and the communion of the Holy Ghost, be with us all. Amen.

(*Or, instead of the foregoing, the following shorter form may be used after reading appropriate Scripture:*)

Let us pray.

O merciful God, Father of our Lord Jesus Christ, who hath said, Blessed are they that mourn, for they shall be comforted, under the shadow of thy judgments we come to thee, and acknowledge thee to be Lord alone. Thou hast entered this house with thy chastenings: O be thou nigh in thy tender compassion to these afflicted ones. Bless thy sorrowing servants with thy consolations, which are neither few nor small. Convert them wholly to thyself, and fill their bleeding hearts with thy love. Make the night of their grief to be light by thy grace. Deliver us, thy servants, we pray thee, from the bondage of our sins, that we may be free from fear of death, and be ready at thy coming. Yea, Lord, do thou sanctify us by thy Holy Spirit, that whether we live, we may live unto the Lord, or whether we die, we may die unto the Lord; so that whether we live or die, we may be the Lord's.

Almighty and everlasting God, we thine unworthy servants, beseech thee, through Christ thy Son, to have mercy upon us. From the borders of the grave we cry unto thee, Have mercy upon us. It hath pleased thee to call out of this world the soul of our departed *brother*, whose body we now follow to *his* burial. We humbly entreat thee that we may with true penitence of heart receive the warning of thy providence, and consider that by reason of our guilt it is appointed unto us to die, and that in a moment when we think not we may appear before thee. Yea, Lord, by reason of our sins we are in the midst of death. Spare us, O Lord; O most pitiful and long-suffering Lord God, spare us a little longer, that we may turn unto thee with true repentance and with lively faith in thy Son Jesus Christ, and when he shall appear we may have confidence, and not be ashamed at his coming. O merciful God, Father of our Lord Jesus Christ, suffer none of us to live without God in the world, not to die without hope; but constrain us mightily by thy love; that we, being renewed by thy grace, and accepted through Christ's intercession, may walk before thee in newness of life, and praise thee forever among the assembly of thy saints, where there shall be no more death, and sorrow and sighing shall flee away; which things we implore in the name of him who has taught us to say:

Our Father, who art in heaven, hallowed be thy name, etc.

BENEDICTION.

The grace of the Lord Jesus Christ, and the love of God, and the communion of the Holy Ghost, be with us all. Amen.

THE PSALTER.

SELECTIONS

FROM THE

PSALMS AND OTHER SCRIPTURES.

FIRST DAY OF THE MONTH.

Morning.

Psalm I.

BLESSED is the man that walketh not in the counsel of the ungodly,

Nor standeth in the way of sinners, nor sitteth in the seat of the scornful.

But his delight is in the law of the Lord;

And in his law doth he meditate day and night.

And he shall be like a tree planted by the rivers of water,

That bringeth forth his fruit in his season;

His leaf also shall not wither;

And whatsoever he doeth shall prosper.

The ungodly are not so:

But are like the chaff which the wind driveth away.

Therefore the ungodly shall not stand in the judgment,

Nor sinners in the congregation of the righteous.

For the LORD knoweth the way of the righteous:
But the way of the ungodly shall perish.

Psalm II.

WHY do the heathen rage,
  And the people imagine a vain thing?
The kings of the earth set themselves,
  And the rulers take counsel together, against the Lord, and against his Anointed, saying,
Let us break their bands asunder,
  And cast away their cords from us.
He that sitteth in the heavens shall laugh:
  The Lord shall have them in derision.
Then shall he speak unto them in his wrath,
  And vex them in his sore displeasure.
Yet have I set my king
  Upon my holy hill of Zion.
I will declare the decree: the LORD hath said unto me, Thou art my son;
  This day have I begotten thee.
Ask of me, and I shall give thee the heathen for thine inheritance,
  And the uttermost parts of the earth for thy possession.
Thou shalt break them with a rod of iron;
  Thou shalt dash them in pieces like a potter's vessel.
Be wise now, therefore, O ye kings:
  Be instructed, ye judges of the earth.

Serve the LORD with fear,
And rejoice with trembling.
Kiss the Son, lest he be angry, and ye perish from the way, when his wrath is kindled but a little.
Blessed are all they that put their trust in him.

FIRST DAY OF THE MONTH.

Afternoon.

PSALM III.

LORD, how are they increased that trouble me?
Many are they that rise up against me.
Many there be which say of my soul,
There is no help for him in God.
But thou, O LORD, art a shield for me;
My glory, and the lifter up of mine head.
I cried unto the LORD with my voice,
And he heard me out of his holy hill.
I laid me down and slept;
I awaked: for the Lord sustained me.
I will not be afraid of ten thousands of people,
That have set themselves against me round about.
Arise, O LORD; save me, O my God; for thou hast smitten all mine enemies upon the cheek bone;
Thou hast broken the teeth of the ungodly.
Salvation belongeth unto the LORD:
Thy blessing is upon thy people.

Psalm IV.

HEAR me when I call, O God of my righteousness:
Thou hast enlarged me when I was in distress;
Have mercy upon me, and hear my prayer.
But know that the LORD hath set apart him that is godly for himself:
The Lord will hear when I call unto him.
Stand in awe, and sin not:
Commune with your own heart upon your bed, and be still.
Offer the sacrifices of righteousness;
And put your trust in the Lord.
There be many that say, Who will show us any good?
Lord, lift thou up the light of thy countenance upon us.
Thou hast put gladness in my heart,
More than in the time that their corn and their wine increased.
I will both lay me down in peace, and sleep:
For thou, Lord, only makest me dwell in safety.

SECOND DAY OF THE MONTH.
Morning.
Psalm V.

GIVE ear to my words, O Lord;
Consider my meditation.
Hearken unto the voice of my cry, my King and my God:
For unto thee will I pray.
My voice shalt thou hear in the morning, O Lord;
In the morning will I direct my prayer unto thee, and will look up.
For thou art not a God that hath pleasure in wickedness;
Neither shall evil dwell with thee.
But as for me, I will come into thy house in the multitude of thy mercy;
And in thy fear will I worship toward thy holy temple.
Lead me, O Lord, in thy righteousness, because of mine enemies;
Make thy way straight before my face.
For there is no faithfulness in their mouth; their inward part is very wickedness.
Their throat is an open sepulchre; they flatter with their tongue.
But let all those that put their trust in thee rejoice: let them ever shout for joy, because thou defendest them:
Let them also that love thy name be joyful in thee.

For thou, LORD, wilt bless the righteous;
With favor wilt thou compass him as with a shield.

Psalm VIII.

O LORD, our LORD, how excellent is thy name in all the earth!
Who hast set thy glory above the heavens.
Out of the mouth of babes and sucklings hast thou ordained strength, because of thine enemies,
That thou mightest still the enemy and the avenger.
When I consider thy heavens, the work of thy fingers,
The moon and the stars, which thou hast ordained;
What is man, that thou art mindful of him?
And the son of man, that thou visitest him?
For thou hast made him a little lower than the angels,
And hast crowned him with glory and honor.
Thou madest him to have dominion over the works of thy hands;
Thou hast put all things under his feet:
All sheep and oxen,
Yea, and the beasts of the field;
The fowl of the air, and the fish of the sea,
And whatsoever passeth through the paths of the seas.
O LORD, our LORD,
How excellent is thy name in all the earth!

SECOND DAY OF THE MONTH.

Afternoon.

Psalm XV.

LORD, who shall abide in thy tabernacle?
Who shall dwell in thy holy hill?
He that walketh uprightly, and worketh righteousness,
And speaketh the truth in his heart.
He that backbiteth not with his tongue, nor doeth evil to his neighbor,
Nor taketh up a reproach against his neighbor.
In whose eyes a vile person is contemned;
But he honoreth them that fear the Lord.
He that sweareth to his own hurt, and changeth not.
He that putteth not out his money to usury,
Nor taketh reward against the innocent.
He that doeth these things shall never be moved.

Psalm XVI.

PRESERVE me, O God:
For in thee do I put my trust.
The LORD is the portion of mine inheritance and of my cup:
Thou maintainest my lot.
The lines are fallen unto me in pleasant places;
Yea, I have a goodly heritage.

I will bless the LORD, who hath given me counsel,
My reins also instruct me in the night seasons.
I have set the LORD always before me:
Because he is at my right hand, I shall not be moved.
Therefore my heart is glad, and my glory rejoiceth·
My flesh also shall rest in hope.
For thou wilt not leave my soul in hell;
Neither wilt thou suffer thine Holy One to see corruption.
Thou wilt show me the path of life: in thy presence is fullness of joy;
At thy right hand there are pleasures for evermore.

THIRD DAY OF THE MONTH.

Morning.

PSALM XVIII.

I WILL love thee, O LORD, my strength.
The Lord is my rock, and my fortress, and my deliverer;
My God, my strength, in whom I will trust;
My buckler, and the horn of my salvation, and my high tower.
I will call upon the LORD, who is worthy to be praised:
So shall I be saved from mine enemies.
In my distress I called upon the LORD,
And cried unto my God:

He heard my voice out of his temple,
And my cry came before him, even into his ears.
Then the earth shook and trembled;
The foundations also of the hills moved and were shaken, because he was wroth.
There went up a smoke out of his nostrils, and fire out of his mouth devoured:
Coals were kindled by it.
He bowed the heavens also, and came down:
And darkness was under his feet.
And he rode upon a cherub, and did fly;
Yea, he did fly upon the wings of the wind.
He made darkness his secret place:
His pavilion round about him were dark waters, and thick clouds of the skies.
At the brightness that was before him his thick clouds passed,
Hail stones and coals of fire.
The LORD also thundered in the heavens, and the Highest gave his voice;
Hail stones and coals of fire.
Yea, he sent out his arrows and scattered them;
And he shot out lightnings, and discomfited them.
Then the channels of waters were seen,
And the foundations of the world were discovered
At thy rebuke, O LORD,
At the blast of the breath of thy nostrils.
He sent from above, he took me,
He drew me out of many waters.

He delivered me from my strong enemy,
And from them which hated me: for they were too strong for me.
They prevented me in the day of my calamity:
But the Lord was my stay.
He brought me forth also into a large place;
He delivered me, because he delighted in me.
The LORD rewarded me according to my righteous- [ness;
According to the cleanness of my hands hath he recompensed me.
For I have kept the ways of the LORD,
And have not wickedly departed from my God.
For all his judgments were before me,
And I did not put away his statutes from me.
I was also upright before him,
And I kept myself from mine iniquity.
Therefore hath the LORD recompensed me according to my righteousness,
According to the cleanness of my hands in his eyesight.
With the merciful thou wilt show thyself merciful;
With an upright man thou wilt show thyself upright;
With the pure thou wilt show thyself pure;
And with the froward thou wilt show thyself froward.
For thou wilt save the afflicted people;
But wilt bring down high looks.
For thou wilt light my candle;
The Lord my God will enlighten my darkness.
For by thee I have run through a troop;
And by my God have I leaped over a wall.

As for God, his way is perfect: the word of the LORD is tried;
He is a buckler to all those that trust in him.
For who is God save the LORD?
Or who is a rock save our God?
It is God that girdeth me with strength,
And maketh my way perfect.
He maketh my feet like hinds' feet,
And setteth me upon my high places.
He teacheth my hands to war,
So that a bow of steel is broken by mine arms.
Thou hast also given me the shield of thy salvation: and thy right hand hath holden me up,
And thy gentleness hath made me great.

THIRD DAY OF THE MONTH.
Afternoon.
PSALM XIX.

THE heavens declare the glory of God;
And the firmament showeth his handywork.
Day unto day uttereth speech,
And night unto night showeth knowledge.
There is no speech nor language,
Where their voice is not heard.
Their line is gone out through all the earth,
And their words to the end of the world.
In them hath he set a tabernacle for the sun, which is as a bridegroom coming out of his chamber,

And rejoiceth as a strong man to run a race.

His going forth is from the end of the heaven, and his circuit unto the ends of it:

And there is nothing hid from the heat thereof.

The law of the LORD is perfect, converting the soul:

The testimony of the Lord is sure, making wise the simple.

The statutes of the LORD are right, rejoicing the heart:

The commandment of the Lord is pure, enlightening the eyes.

The fear of the LORD is clean, enduring for ever:

The judgments of the Lord are true and righteous altogether.

More to be desired are they than gold, yea, than much fine gold:

Sweeter also than honey and the honeycomb.

Moreover by them is thy servant warned: and in keeping of them there is great reward.

Who can understand his errors? cleanse thou me from secret faults.

Keep back thy servant also from presumptuous sins; let them not have dominion over me:

Then shall I be upright, and I shall be innocent from the great transgression.

Let the words of my mouth, and the meditation of my heart, be acceptable in thy sight,

O Lord, my strength, and my redeemer.

FOURTH DAY OF THE MONTH.

Morning.

Psalm XX.

THE Lord hear thee in the day of trouble;
The name of the God of Jacob defend thee;
Send thee help from the sanctuary,
And strengthen thee out of Zion;
Remember all thy offerings,
And accept thy burnt sacrifice;
Grant thee according to thine own heart,
And fulfill all thy counsel.
We will rejoice in thy salvation, and in the name of our God we will set up our banners:
The Lord fulfill all thy petitions.
Now know I that the Lord saveth his anointed;
He will hear him from his holy heaven with the saving strength of his right hand.
Some trust in chariots, and some in horses:
But we will remember the name of the Lord our God.
They are brought down and fallen:
But we are risen and stand upright.
Save, Lord:
Let the king hear us when we call.

Psalm XXIII.

THE LORD is my shepherd;
   I shall not want.
He maketh me to lie down in green pastures:
He leadeth me beside the still waters.
He restoreth my soul:
He leadeth me in the paths of righteousness, for his name's sake.
Yea, though I walk through the valley of the shadow of death, I will fear no evil: for thou art with me:
Thy rod and thy staff they comfort me.
Thou preparest a table before me in the presence of mine enemies:
Thou anointest my head with oil; my cup runneth over.
Surely goodness and mercy shall follow me all the days of my life:
And I will dwell in the house of the Lord for ever.

FOURTH DAY OF THE MONTH.
Afternoon.

Psalm XXIV.

THE earth is the LORD's and the fulness thereof;
   The world, and they that dwell therein.
For he hath founded it upon the seas,
And established it upon the floods.

Who shall ascend into the hill of the LORD?
Or who shall stand in his holy place?
He that hath clean hands, and a pure heart;
Who hath not lifted up his soul unto vanity, nor sworn deceitfully.
He shall receive the blessing from the LORD,
And righteousness from the God of his salvation.
This is the generation of them that seek him,
That seek thy face, O Jacob.
Lift up your heads, O ye gates; and be ye lift up, ye everlasting doors;
And the King of glory shall come in.
Who is this King of glory?
The Lord strong and mighty, the Lord mighty in battle.
Lift up your heads, O ye gates; even lift them up, ye everlasting doors;
And the King of glory shall come in.
Who is this King of glory?
The Lord of hosts, He is the King of glory.

PSALM XXV.

UNTO thee, O LORD, do I lift up my soul.
    O my God, I trust in thee:
Let me not be ashamed;
Let not mine enemies triumph over me.

Yea, let none that wait on thee be ashamed:
Let them be ashamed which transgress without cause.
Show me thy ways, O Lord;
Teach me thy paths.
Lead me in thy truth, and teach me:
For thou art the God of my salvation;
On thee do I wait all the day.
Remember, O Lord, thy tender mercies and thy loving-kindnesses;
For they have been ever of old.
Remember not the sins of my youth, nor my transgressions:
According to thy mercy remember thou me,
For thy goodness' sake, O Lord.
Good and upright is the Lord:
Therefore will he teach sinners in the way.
The meek will he guide in judgment:
And the meek will he teach his way.
All the paths of the Lord are mercy and truth
Unto such as keep his covenant and his testimonies.
For thy name's sake, O Lord, pardon mine iniquity;
For it is great.
What man is he that feareth the Lord?
Him shall he teach in the way that he shall choose.
His soul shall dwell at ease;
And his seed shall inherit the earth.
The secret of the Lord is with them that fear him;
And he will show them his covenant.

Mine eyes are ever toward the LORD;
For he shall pluck my feet out of the net.
Turn thee unto me, and have mercy upon me;
O bring thou me out of my distresses:
Look upon mine affliction, and my pain;
And forgive all my sins.
O keep my soul, and deliver me;
Let me not be ashamed; for I put my trust in thee.
Let integrity and uprightness preserve me;
For I wait on thee.

FIFTH DAY OF THE MONTH.

Morning.

PSALM XXVII.

THE LORD is my light and my salvation; whom shall I fear?

The Lord is the strength of my life; of whom shall I be afraid?

Though a host should encamp against me, my heart shall not fear;

Though war should rise against me, in this will I be confident.

One thing have I desired of the LORD, that will I seek after; that I may dwell in the house of the LORD all the days of my life,

To behold the beauty of the Lord, and to inquire in his temple.

For in the time of trouble he shall hide me in his pavilion: in the secret of his tabernacle shall he hide me:

He shall set me up upon a rock.

And now shall mine head be lifted up above mine enemies round about me: therefore will I offer in his tabernacle sacrifices of joy;

I will sing, yea, I will sing praises unto the Lord.

Hear, O Lord, when I cry with my voice:

Have mercy also upon me, and answer me.

When thou saidst, Seek ye my face;

My heart said unto thee, Thy face, Lord, will I seek.

Hide not thy face far from me; put not thy servant away in anger:

Thou hast been my help; leave me not, neither forsake me, O God of my salvation.

When my father and my mother forsake me,

Then the Lord will take me up.

Teach me thy way, O Lord,

And lead me in a plain path, because of mine enemies.

I had fainted unless I had believed to see the goodness of the Lord in the land of the living.

Wait on the Lord.

Be of good courage, and he shall strengthen thine heart:

Wait, I say, on the Lord.

FIFTH DAY OF THE MONTH.
Afternoon.

Psalm XXXI.

IN thee, O Lord, do I put my trust;
Let me never be ashamed:
Deliver me in thy righteousness.
Bow down thine ear to me; deliver me speedily:
Be thou my strong rock, for an house of defence to save me.
For thou art my rock and my fortress:
I will be glad and rejoice in thy mercy:
For thou hast considered my trouble;
Thou hast known my soul in adversities,
And hast not shut me up into the hand of the enemy:
Have mercy upon me, O Lord, for I am in trouble;
Mine eye is consumed with grief,
My strength faileth because of mine iniquity,
But I trusted in thee, O Lord: I said, Thou art my God.
My times are in thy hand:
Deliver me from the hand of mine enemies, and from them that persecute me.
Make thy face to shine upon thy servant:
Save me for thy mercies' sake.
Oh how great is thy goodness,
Which thou hast laid up for them that fear thee;
Thou shalt hide them in the secret of thy presence from the pride of man;

Thou shalt keep them secretly in a pavilion from the strife of tongues.

For I said in my haste, I am cut off from before thine eyes:

Nevertheless thou heardest the voice of my supplications when I cried unto thee.

O love the LORD, all ye his saints;

For the Lord preserveth the faithful, and plentifully rewardeth the proud doer.

Be of good courage, and he shall strengthen your heart,

All ye that hope in the Lord.

SIXTH DAY OF THE MONTH.

Morning.

PSALM XXIX.

GIVE unto the LORD, O ye mighty,
Give unto the Lord, glory and strength.
Give unto the LORD the glory due unto his name;
Worship the Lord in the beauty of holiness.
The voice of the LORD is upon the waters:
The God of glory thundereth: the Lord is upon many waters.
The voice of the LORD is powerful;
The voice of the Lord is full of majesty.
The LORD will give strength unto his people;
The Lord will bless his people with peace.

Psalm XXXIII.

REJOICE in the LORD, O ye righteous:
For praise is comely for the upright.
Praise the LORD with harp:
Sing unto him with the psaltery, and an instrument of ten strings.
Sing unto him a new song;
Play skilfully with a loud noise.
For the word of the LORD is right;
And all his works are done in truth.
He loveth righteousness and judgment:
The earth is full of the goodness of the Lord.
By the word of the LORD were the heavens made:
And all the hosts of them by the breath of his mouth.
He gathereth the waters of the sea together as an heap:
He layeth up the depth in storehouses.
Let all the earth fear the LORD:
Let all the inhabitants of the world stand in awe of him.
For he spake and it was done;
He commanded, and it stood fast.
The LORD bringeth the counsel of the heathen to nought:
He maketh the devices of the people of none effect.
The counsel of the LORD standeth for ever,
The thoughts of his heart to all generations.

Blessed is the nation whose God is the Lord;
And the people whom he hath chosen for his own inheritance.
The Lord looketh from heaven;
He beholdeth all the sons of men.
From the place of his habitation he looketh
Upon all the inhabitants of the earth.
Behold, the eye of the Lord is upon them that fear him,
Upon them that hope in his mercy;
To deliver their soul from death,
And to keep them alive in famine.
Our soul waiteth for the Lord;
He is our help and our shield.
For our heart shall rejoice in him;
Because we have trusted in his holy name.
Let thy mercy, O Lord, be upon us,
According as we hope in thee.

SIXTH DAY OF THE MONTH.

Afternoon.

Psalm XXXIV.

I WILL bless the Lord at all times:
His praise shall continually be in my mouth.
My soul shall make her boast in the Lord:
The humble shall hear thereof, and be glad.

O magnify the LORD with me,
And let us exalt his name together.
I sought the LORD, and he heard me,
And delivered me from all my fears.
They looked unto him and were lightened;
And their faces were not ashamed.
This poor man cried, and the LORD heard him,
And saved him out of all his troubles.
The angel of the LORD encampeth round about them that fear him,
And delivereth them.
O taste and see that the LORD is good:
Blessed is the man that trusteth in him.
O fear the LORD, ye his saints·
For there is no want to them that fear him.
The young lions do lack and suffer hunger:
But they that seek the Lord shall not want any good thing.
Come, ye children, hearken unto me:
I will teach you the fear of the Lord.
What man is he that desireth life,
And loveth many days, that he may see good?
Keep thy tongue from evil,
And thy lips from speaking guile.
Depart from evil, and do good;
Seek peace, and pursue it.
The eyes of the LORD are upon the righteous,
And his ears are open unto their cry.
The face of the LORD is against them that do evil,

To cut off the remembrance of them from the earth.
The righteous cry, and the LORD heareth,
And delivereth them out of all their troubles.
The LORD is nigh unto them that are of a broken heart;
And saveth such as be of a contrite spirit.
Many are the afflictions of the righteous:
But the Lord delivereth him out of them all.
He keepeth all his bones:
Not one of them is broken.
Evil shall slay the wicked;
And they that hate the righteous shall be desolate.
The LORD redeemeth the soul of his servants;
And none of them that trust in him shall be desolate.

SEVENTH DAY OF THE MONTH.
𝔐orning.

PSALM XXXVI.

THY mercy, O LORD, is in the heavens,
And thy faithfulness reacheth unto the clouds.
Thy righteousness is like the great mountains: thy judgments are a great deep:
O Lord, thou preservest man and beast.
How excellent is thy loving-kindness, O God!
Therefore the children of men put their trust under the shadow of thy wings.

They shall be abundantly satisfied with the fatness of thy house;
And thou shalt make them drink of the river of thy pleasures.
For with thee is the fountain of life:
In thy light shall we see light.
O continue thy loving kindness unto them that know thee;
And thy righteousness to the upright in heart.
Let not the foot of pride come against me,
And let not the hand of the wicked remove me.

Psalm XXXVII.

FRET not thyself because of evil doers,
Neither be thou envious against the workers of iniquity.
For they shall soon be cut down like the grass,
And wither as the green herb.
Trust in the LORD, and do good:
So shalt thou dwell in the land, and verily thou shalt be fed.
Delight thyself also in the LORD;
And he shall give thee the desires of thine heart.
Commit thy way unto the LORD;
Trust also in him, and he shall bring it to pass:
And he shall bring forth thy righteousness as the light,

And thy judgment as the noonday.

Rest in the Lord, and wait patiently for him:
Fret not thyself because of him who prospereth in his way, because of the man who bringeth wicked devices to pass.

Cease from anger, and forsake wrath;
Fret not thyself in any wise to do evil.

For evil doers shall be cut off:
But those that wait upon the Lord, they shall inherit the earth.

For yet a little while, and the wicked shall not be;
Yea, thou shalt diligently consider his place, and it shall not be.

But the meek shall inherit the earth,
And shall delight themselves in the abundance of peace.

The steps of a good man are ordered by the Lord;
And he delighteth in his way.

Though he fall, he shall not be utterly cast down:
For the Lord upholdeth him with his hand.

I have been young, and now am old;
Yet have I not seen the righteous forsaken, nor his seed begging bread.

He is ever merciful, and lendeth;
And his seed is blessed.

Depart from evil, and do good;
And dwell for evermore.

For the Lord loveth judgment,
And forsaketh not his saints.

The mouth of the righteous speaketh wisdom,
And his tongue talketh of judgment.
The law of his God is in his heart:
None of his steps shall slide.
Mark the perfect man, and behold the upright:
For the end of that man is peace.
The salvation of the righteous is of the LORD;
He is their strength in the time of trouble.
And the LORD shall help them, and deliver them;
He shall deliver them from the wicked, and save them, because they trust in him.

SEVENTH DAY OF THE MONTH.

Afternoon.

PSALM XLII.

AS the hart panteth after the water brooks,
So panteth my soul after thee, O God.
My soul thirsteth for God, for the living God:
When shall I come and appear before God?
My tears have been my meat day and night,
While they continually say unto me, Where is thy God?
When I remember these things, I pour out my soul in me: for I had gone with the multitude; I went with them to the house of God,
With the voice of joy and praise, with a multitude that kept holyday.

Why art thou cast down, O my soul? and why art thou disquieted in me?

Hope thou in God; for I shall yet praise him for the help of his countenance.

O my God, my soul is cast down within me: therefore will I remember thee,

From the land of Jordan, and of the Hermonites, from the hill Mizar.

Deep calleth unto deep at the noise of thy waterspouts:

All thy waves and thy billows are gone over me.

Yet the LORD will command his loving-kindness in the daytime,

And in the night his song shall be with me, and my prayer unto the God of my life.

I will say unto God my rock, Why hast thou forgotten me?

Why go I mourning because of the oppression of the enemy?

As with a sword in my bones, mine enemies reproach me;

While they say daily unto me, Where is thy God?

Why art thou cast down, O my soul? and why art thou disquieted within me?

Hope thou in God; for I shall yet praise him, who is the health of my countenance, and my God.

EIGHTH DAY OF THE MONTH.

Morning.

Psalm XLIII.

JUDGE me, O God, and plead my cause against an ungodly nation:

O deliver me from the deceitful and unjust man.

For thou art the God of my strength: why dost thou cast me off?

Why go I mourning because of the oppression of the enemy?

Oh send out thy light and thy truth: let them lead me;

Let them bring me unto thy holy hill, and to thy tabernacles.

Then will I go unto the altar of God, unto God my exceeding joy:

Yea, upon the harp will I praise thee, O God, my God.

Why art thou cast down, O my soul? and why art thou disquieted within me?

Hope in God; for I shall yet praise him, who is the health of my countenance, and my God.

Psalm XLV.

MY heart is inditing a good matter: I speak of the things which I have made touching the king:
My tongue is the pen of a ready writer.
Thou art fairer than the children of men; grace is poured into thy lips:
Therefore God hath blessed thee for ever.
Gird thy sword upon thy thigh, O most mighty,
With thy glory and thy majesty.
And in thy majesty ride prosperously, because of truth and meekness and righteousness;
And thy right hand shall teach thee terrible things.
Thine arrows are sharp in the heart of the king's enemies;
Whereby the people fall under thee.
Thy throne, O God, is for ever and ever:
The sceptre of thy kingdom is a right sceptre.
Thou lovest righteousness, and hatest wickedness:
Therefore God, thy God, hath anointed thee with the oil of gladness above thy fellows.
I will make thy name to be remembered in all generations;
Therefore shall the people praise thee for ever and ever.

EIGHTH DAY OF THE MONTH.

Afternoon.

Psalm XLVI.

GOD is our refuge and strength,
A very present help in trouble.
Therefore will not we fear, though the earth be removed,
And though the mountains be carried into the midst of the sea;
Though the waters thereof roar and be troubled,
Though the mountains shake with the swelling thereof.
There is a river, the streams whereof shall make glad the city of God;
The holy place of the tabernacles of the Most High.
God is in the midst of her; she shall not be moved:
God shall help her, and that right early.
The heathen raged, the kingdoms were moved:
He uttered his voice, the earth melted.
The Lord of hosts is with us;
The God of Jacob is our refuge.
Come, behold the works of the Lord,
What desolations he hath made in the earth.
He maketh wars to cease unto the end of the earth;
He breaketh the bow, and cutteth the spear in sunder: he burneth the chariot in the fire.

Be still, and know that I am God;
I will be exalted among the heathen, I will be exalted in the earth.
The LORD of hosts is with us;
The God of Jacob is our refuge.

PSALM XLVII.

O CLAP your hands, all ye people:
Shout unto God with the voice of triumph.
For the LORD most high is terrible;
He is a great King over all the earth.
He shall choose our inheritance for us,
The excellency of Jacob whom he loved.
God is gone up with a shout,
The Lord with the sound of a trumpet.
Sing praises to God, sing praises;
Sing praises unto our King, sing praises.
For God is the King of all the earth:
Sing ye praises with understanding.
God reigneth over the heathen:
God sitteth upon the throne of his holiness.

NINTH DAY OF THE MONTH.

Morning.

Psalm XLVIII.

GREAT is the LORD, and greatly to be praised
In the city of our God, in the mountain of his holiness.

Beautiful for situation, the joy of the whole earth, is Mount Zion,
On the sides of the north, the city of the great King.

God is known in her palaces for a refuge.
For, lo, the kings were assembled, they passed by together.

They saw it, and so they marvelled;
They were troubled, and hasted away.

As we have heard, so have we seen in the city of the Lord of hosts, in the city of our God:
God will establish it for ever.

We have thought of thy loving-kindness, O God,
In the midst of thy temple.

According to thy name, O God, so is thy praise, unto the ends of the earth:
Thy right hand is full of righteousness.

Let Mount Zion rejoice,
Let the daughters of Judah be glad, because of thy judgments.

Walk about Zion, and go round about her:
Tell the towers thereof.

Mark ye well her bulwarks, consider her palaces:
That ye may tell it to the generation following.
For this God is our God for ever and ever;
He will be our guide even unto death.

NINTH DAY OF THE MONTH.

Afternoon.

Psalm LI.

HAVE mercy upon me, O God, according to thy loving-kindness;
According unto the multitude of thy tender mercies blot out my transgressions.
Wash me throughly from mine iniquity,
And cleanse me from my sin.
For I acknowledge my transgressions;
And my sin is ever before me.
Against thee, thee only, have I sinned,
And done this evil in thy sight;
That thou mightest be justified when thou speakest,
And be clear when thou judgest.
Behold, thou desirest truth in the inward parts;
And in the hidden part thou shalt make me to know wisdom.
Purge me with hyssop, and I shall be clean:
Wash me, and I shall be whiter than snow.

Make me to hear joy and gladness;
That the bones which thou hast broken may rejoice.
Hide thy face from my sins,
And blot out all mine iniquities.
Create in me a clean heart, O God;
And renew a right spirit within me.
Cast me not away from thy presence;
And take not thy Holy Spirit from me.
Restore unto me the joy of thy salvation;
And uphold me with thy free Spirit.
Then will I teach transgressors thy ways;
And sinners shall be converted unto thee.
Deliver me from blood guiltiness, O God, thou God of my salvation;
And my tongue shall sing aloud of thy righteousness.
O LORD, open thou my lips;
And my mouth shall show forth thy praise.
For thou desirest not sacrifice, else would I give it;
Thou delightest not in burnt offering.
The sacrifices of God are a broken spirit:
A broken and a contrite heart, O God, thou wilt not despise.
Do good in thy good pleasure unto Zion:
Build thou the walls of Jerusalem.
Then shalt thou be pleased with the sacrifices of righteousness, with burnt offering and whole burnt offering;
Then shall they offer bullocks upon thine altar.

TENTH DAY OF THE MONTH.
Morning.
Psalm CXXX.

OUT of the depths have I cried unto thee, O Lord.
Lord, hear my voice;
Let thine ears be attentive
To the voice of my supplications.
If thou, Lord, shouldest mark iniquities,
O Lord, who shall stand?
But there is forgiveness with thee,
That thou mayest be feared.
I wait for the Lord, my soul doth wait,
And in his word do I hope.
My soul waiteth for the Lord more than they that watch for the morning:
I say, more than they that watch for the morning.
Let Israel hope in the Lord: for with the Lord there is mercy,
And with him is plenteous redemption.
And he shall redeem Israel
From all his iniquities.

Psalm LV.

GIVE ear to my prayer, O God;
And hide not thyself from my supplication.
Attend unto me, and hear me:

I mourn in my complaint, and make a noise;

Because of the voice of the enemy, because of the oppression of the wicked:

For they cast iniquity upon me, and in wrath they hate me.

My heart is sore pained within me;

And the terrors of death are fallen upon me.

Fearfulness and trembling are come upon me,

And horror hath overwhelmed me.

And I said, Oh that I had wings like a dove!

For then would I fly away and be at rest.

Lo, then would I wander far off,

And remain in the wilderness.

As for me, I will call upon God;

And the Lord shall save me.

Evening, and morning, and at noon, will I pray, and cry aloud;

And he shall hear my voice.

He hath delivered my soul in peace from the battle that was against me:

For there were many with me.

God shall hear and afflict them,

Even he that abideth of old.

Because they have no changes,

Therefore they fear not God.

Cast thy burden upon the LORD, and he shall sustain thee:

He shall never suffer the righteous to be moved.

TENTH DAY OF THE MONTH.

Afternoon.

Psalm LVII.

BE merciful unto me, O God, be merciful unto me:
For my soul trusteth in thee:
Yea, in the shadow of thy wings will I make my refuge,
Until these calamities be overpast.
I will cry unto God most high;
Unto God that performeth all things for me.
He shall send from heaven, and save me
From the reproach of him that would swallow me up.
Be thou exalted, O God, above the heavens;
Let thy glory be above all the earth.
My heart is fixed, O God, my heart is fixed:
I will sing and give praise.
Awake up, my glory; awake, psaltery and harp;
I myself will awake early.
I will praise thee, O LORD, among the people;
I will sing unto thee among the nations.
For thy mercy is great unto the heavens,
And thy truth unto the clouds.
Be thou exalted, O God, above the heavens:
Let thy glory be above all the earth.

Psalm LXI.

HEAR my cry, O God;
Attend unto my prayer.
From the end of the earth will I cry unto thee, when my heart is overwhelmed:
Lead me to the rock that is higher than I.
For thou hast been a shelter for me,
And a strong tower from the enemy.
I will abide in thy tabernacle for ever;
I will trust in the covert of thy wings.
For thou, O God, hast heard my vows:
Thou hast given me the heritage of those that fear thy name.
So will I sing praise unto thy name for ever,
That I may daily perform my vows.

ELEVENTH DAY OF THE MONTH.

Morning.

Psalm LXII.

TRULY my soul waiteth upon God:
From him cometh my salvation.
He only is my rock and my salvation;
He is my defence: I shall not be greatly moved.
My soul, wait thou only upon God:
For my expectation is from him.

He only is my rock and my salvation;
He is my defence: I shall not be moved.
In God is my salvation and my glory:
The rock of my strength, and my refuge, is in God.
Trust in him at all times; ye people, pour out your heart before him:
God is a refuge for us.
Surely men of low degree are vanity, and men of high degree are a lie:
To be laid in the balance, they are altogether lighter than vanity.
Trust not in oppression, and become not vain in robbery:
If riches increase, set not your heart upon them.
God hath spoken once; twice have I heard this;
That power belongeth unto God.
Also unto thee, O LORD, belongeth mercy:
For thou renderest to every man according to his work.

Psalm LXIII.

O GOD, thou art my God; early will I seek thee; my soul thirsteth for thee,
My flesh longeth for thee in a dry and thirsty land, where no water is;
To see thy power and thy glory,
So as I have seen thee in the sanctuary.
Because thy loving-kindness is better than life,

My lips shall praise thee.
Thus will I bless thee while I live:
I will lift up my hands in thy name.
My soul shall be satisfied as with marrow and fatness;
And my mouth shall praise thee with joyful lips:
When I remember thee upon my bed,
And meditate on thee in the night watches.
Because thou hast been my help,
Therefore in the shadow of thy wings will I rejoice.
My soul followeth hard after thee:
Thy right hand upholdeth me.

ELEVENTH DAY OF THE MONTH.

Afternoon.

Psalm LXV.

PRAISE waiteth for thee, O God, in Zion:
And unto thee shall the vow be performed.
O thou that hearest prayer, unto thee shall all flesh come.
Iniquities prevail against me: as for our transgressions, thou shalt purge them away.
Blessed is the man whom thou choosest, and causest to approach unto thee, that he may dwell in thy courts:
We shall be satisfied with the goodness of thy house, even of thy holy temple.

By terrible things in righteousness wilt thou answer us, O God of our salvation;
Who art the confidence of all the ends of the earth, and of them that are afar off upon the sea:
Which by his strength setteth fast the mountains; being girded with power:
Which stilleth the noise of the seas, the noise of their waves, and the tumult of the people.
They also that dwell in the uttermost parts are afraid at thy tokens:
Thou makest the outgoings of the morning and evening to rejoice.
Thou visitest the earth, and waterest it:
Thou greatly enrichest it
With the river of God, which is full of water:
Thou preparest them corn, when thou hast so provided for it.
Thou waterest the ridges thereof abundantly, thou settlest the furrows thereof:
Thou makest it soft with showers, thou blessest the springing thereof.
Thou crownest the year with thy goodness;
And thy paths drop fatness.
They drop upon the pastures of the wilderness:
And the little hills rejoice on every side.
The pastures are clothed with flocks;
The valleys also are covered over with corn; they shout for joy, they also sing.

TWELFTH DAY OF THE MONTH.

Morning.

Psalm LXVI.

MAKE a joyful noise unto God, all ye lands:
Sing forth the honor of his name: make his praise glorious.
All the earth shall worship thee, and shall sing unto thee;
They shall sing to thy name.
He turned the sea into dry land: they went through the flood on foot:
There did we rejoice in him.
He ruleth by his power for ever: his eyes behold the nations:
Let not the rebellious exalt themselves.
O bless our God, ye people,
And make the voice of his praise to be heard:
Which holdeth our soul in life,
And suffereth not our feet to be moved.
For thou, O God, hast proved us:
Thou hast tried us, as silver is tried.
I will go into thy house with burnt offerings:
I will pay thee my vows,
Which my lips have uttered,
And my mouth hath spoken, when I was in trouble.
Come and hear, all ye that fear God,
And I will declare what he hath done for my soul.

I cried unto him with my mouth,
And he was extolled with my tongue.
If I regard iniquity in my heart,
The Lord will not hear me:
But verily God hath heard me;
He hath attended to the voice of my prayer.
Blessed be God, which hath not turned away my prayer,
Nor his mercy from me.

TWELFTH DAY OF THE MONTH.

Afternoon.

Psalm LXVII.

GOD be merciful unto us, and bless us;
And cause his face to shine upon us.
That thy way may be known upon earth,
Thy saving health among all nations.
Let the people praise thee, O God;
Let all the people praise thee.
O let the nations be glad and sing for joy: for thou shalt judge the people righteously,
And govern the nations upon earth.
Let the people praise thee, O God;
Let all the people praise thee.
Then shall the earth yield her increase;
And God, even our own God, shall bless us.

God shall bless us,
And all the ends of the earth shall fear him.

Psalm LXVIII.

A FATHER of the fatherless, and a judge of the widows,
Is God in his holy habitation.
God setteth the solitary in families: he bringeth out those which are bound with chains:
But the rebellious dwell in a dry land.
O God, when thou wentest forth before thy people,
When thou didst march through the wilderness;
The earth shook, the heavens also dropped at the presence of God:
Even Sinai itself was moved at the presence of God, the God of Israel.
The chariots of God are twenty thousand, even thousands of angels:
The Lord is among them, as in Sinai, in the holy place.
Thou hast ascended on high, thou hast led captivity captive: thou hast received gifts for men;
Yea, for the rebellious also, that the Lord God might dwell among them.
Blessed be the Lord, who daily loadeth us with benefits,
Even the God of our salvation.

THIRTEENTH DAY OF THE MONTH.

Morning.

Psalm LXXI.

IN thee, O Lord, do I put my trust;
Let me never be put to confusion.
Deliver me in thy righteousness, and cause me to escape:
Incline thine ear unto me, and save me.
Be thou my strong habitation, whereunto I may continually resort:
Thou hast given commandment to save me: for thou art my rock and my fortress.
Deliver me, O my God, out of the hand of the wicked,
Out of the hand of the unrighteous and cruel man.
For thou art my hope, O Lord God:
Thou art my trust from my youth.
I am as a wonder unto many;
But thou art my strong refuge.
Let my mouth be filled with thy praise
And with thy honor all the day.
Cast me not off in the time of old age;
Forsake me not when my strength faileth.
O God, be not far from me:
O my God, make haste for my help.
But I will hope continually,
And will yet praise thee more and more.

My mouth shall show forth thy righteousness
And thy salvation all the day.
I will go in the strength of the Lord God:
I will make mention of thy righteousness, even of thine only.
O God, thou hast taught me from my youth:
And hitherto have I declared thy wondrous works.
Thy righteousness also, O God, is very high,
Who hast done great things: O God, who is like unto thee?
I will also praise thee with the psaltery,
Even thy truth, O my God:
Unto thee will I sing with the harp,
O thou Holy One of Israel.
My lips shall greatly rejoice when I sing unto thee;
And my soul, which thou hast redeemed.
My tongue also shall talk of thy righteousness
All the day long.

THIRTEENTH DAY OF THE MONTH.

Afternoon.

Psalm LXXII.

GIVE the king thy judgments, O God,
And thy righteousness unto the king's son.
He shall judge thy people with righteousness,
And thy poor with judgment.

The mountains shall bring peace to the people,
And the little hills, by righteousness.
He shall judge the poor of the people,
He shall save the children of the needy, and shall break in pieces the oppressor.
They shall fear thee as long as the sun and moon endure,
Throughout all generations.
He shall come down like rain upon the mown grass:
As showers that water the earth.
In his days shall the righteous flourish:
And abundance of peace so long as the moon endureth.
He shall have dominion also from sea to sea,
And from the river unto the ends of the earth.
They that dwell in the wilderness shall bow before him;
And his enemies shall lick the dust.
The kings of Tarshish and of the isles shall bring presents:
The kings of Sheba and Seba shall offer gifts.
Yea, all kings shall fall down before him:
All nations shall serve him.
For he shall deliver the needy when he crieth;
The poor also, and him that hath no helper.
He shall spare the poor and needy,
And shall save the souls of the needy.
He shall redeem their soul from deceit and violence:
And precious shall their blood be in his sight.

And he shall live, and to him shall be given of the gold of Sheba:

Prayer also shall be made for him continually; and daily shall he be praised.

There shall be an handful of corn in the earth upon the top of the mountains; the fruit thereof shall shake like Lebanon:

And they of the city shall flourish like grass of the earth.

His name shall endure for ever: his name shall be continued as long as the sun:

And men shall be blessed in him: all nations shall call him blessed.

Blessed be the LORD God, the God of Israel,

Who only doeth wondrous things.

And blessed be his glorious name for ever:

And let the whole earth be filled with his glory. Amen, and Amen.

FOURTEENTH DAY OF THE MONTH.

Morning.

PSALM LXXX.

GIVE ear, O Shepherd of Israel, thou that leadest Joseph like a flock;

Thou that dwellest between the cherubim, shine forth.

Before Ephraim and Benjamin and Manasseh stir up thy strength,
And come and save us.
Turn us again, O God,
And cause thy face to shine; and we shall be saved.
Thou hast brought a vine out of Egypt:
Thou hast cast out the heathen, and planted it.
Thou preparedst room before it,
And didst cause it to take deep root, and it filled the land.
The hills were covered with the shadow of it,
And the boughs thereof were like the goodly cedars.
She sent out her boughs unto the sea,
And her branches unto the river.
Return, we beseech thee, O God of hosts:
Look down from heaven, and behold, and visit this vine;
And the vineyard which thy right hand hath planted,
And the branch that thou madest strong for thyself.
Let thy hand be upon the man of thy right hand,
Upon the son of man whom thou madest strong for thyself.
So will not we go back from thee:
Quicken us, and we will call upon thy name.
Turn us again, O LORD God of hosts,
Cause thy face to shine; and we shall be saved.

FOURTEENTH DAY OF THE MONTH.
Afternoon.
Psalm LXXXIV.

How amiable are thy tabernacles,
 O Lord of hosts!
My soul longeth, yea, even fainteth for the courts of the Lord:
My heart and my flesh crieth out for the living God.
Yea, the sparrow hath found an house,
And the swallow a nest for herself, where she may lay her young,
Even thine altars, O Lord of hosts,
My King and my God.
Blessed are they that dwell in thy house:
They will be still praising thee.
They go from strength to strength,
Every one of them in Zion appeareth before God.
O Lord God of hosts, hear my prayer:
Give ear, O God of Jacob.
Behold, O God our shield,
And look upon the face of thine anointed.
For the Lord God is a sun and shield: the Lord will give grace and glory;
No good thing will he withhold from them that walk uprightly.
O Lord of hosts,
Blessed is the man that trusteth in thee.

Psalm LXXXV.

LORD, thou hast been favorable unto thy land :
Thou hast brought back the captivity of Jacob.
Thou hast forgiven the iniquity of thy people ;
Thou hast covered all their sin.
Show us thy mercy, O LORD,
And grant us thy salvation.
I will hear what God the LORD will speak : for he will speak peace unto his people, and to his saints :
But let them not turn again to folly.
Surely his salvation is nigh them that fear him ;
That glory may dwell in our land.
Mercy and truth are met together ;
Righteousness and peace have kissed each other.
Truth shall spring out of the earth ;
And righteousness shall look down from heaven.
Yea, the LORD shall give that which is good ;
And our land shall yield her increase.
Righteousness shall go before him ;
And shall set us in the way of his steps.

FIFTEENTH DAY OF THE MONTH.

Morning.

Psalm LXXXVI.

BOW down thine ear, O LORD, hear me :
For I am poor and needy.
Preserve my soul ; for I am holy :

O thou my God, save thy servant that trusteth in thee.
Be merciful unto me, O Lord:
For I cry unto thee daily.
Rejoice the soul of thy servant:
For unto thee, O Lord, do I lift up my soul.
For thou, Lord, art good, and ready to forgive;
And plenteous in mercy unto all them that call upon thee.
Give ear, O Lord, unto my prayer;
And attend to the voice of my supplications.
In the day of my trouble I will call upon thee:
For thou wilt answer me.
All nations whom thou hast made shall come and worship before thee, O Lord;
And shall glorify thy name.
For thou art great, and doest wondrous things:
Thou art God alone.
Teach me thy way, O Lord; I will walk in thy truth:
Unite my heart to fear thy name.
I will praise thee, O Lord my God, with all my heart:
And I will glorify thy name for evermore.
But thou, O Lord, art a God full of compassion, and gracious,
Longsuffering, and plenteous in mercy and truth.
O turn unto me, and have mercy upon me;
Give thy strength unto thy servant, and save the son of thine handmaid.

Psalm LXXXVII.

HIS foundation is in the holy mountains. The LORD loveth the gates of Zion
More than all the dwellings of Jacob.
Glorious things are spoken of thee,
O city of God.
And of Zion it shall be said, This and that man was born in her:
And the highest himself shall establish her.
The LORD shall count, when he writeth up the people,
That this man was born there.
As well the singers as the players on instruments shall be there:
All my springs are in thee.

FIFTEENTH DAY OF THE MONTH.
Afternoon.

Psalm LXXXIX.

I WILL sing of the mercies of the LORD for ever:
With my mouth will I make known thy faithfulness to all generations.
For I have said, Mercy shall be built up for ever:
Thy faithfulness shalt thou establish in the very heavens.

For who in the heaven can be compared unto the Lord?

Who among the sons of the mighty can be likened unto the Lord?

God is greatly to be feared in the assembly of the saints,

And to be had in reverence of all them that are about him.

O Lord God of hosts, who is a strong Lord like unto thee?

Or to thy faithfulness round about thee?

Thou rulest the raging of the sea:

When the waves thereof arise, thou stillest them.

The heavens are thine, the earth also is thine:

As for the world and the fulness thereof, thou hast founded them.

The north and the south thou hast created them:

Tabor and Hermon shall rejoice in thy name.

Thou hast a mighty arm:

Strong is thy hand, and high is thy right hand.

Justice and judgment are the habitation of thy throne:

Mercy and truth shall go before thy face.

Blessed is the people that know the joyful sound:

They shall walk, O Lord, in the light of thy countenance.

In thy name shall they rejoice all the day:

And in thy righteousness shall they be exalted.

SIXTEENTH DAY OF THE MONTH.

Morning.

Psalm XC.

LORD, thou hast been our dwelling-place
In all generations.
Before the mountains were brought forth, or ever thou hadst formed the earth and the world,
Even from everlasting to everlasting, thou art God.
Thou turnest man to destruction;
And sayest, Return, ye children of men.
For a thousand years in thy sight are but as yesterday when it is past,
And as a watch in the night.
Thou carriest them away as with a flood; they are as a sleep;
In the morning they are like grass which groweth up.
In the morning it flourisheth, and groweth up;
In the evening it is cut down, and withereth.
For we are consumed by thine anger,
And by thy wrath are we troubled.
Thou hast set our iniquities before thee,
Our secret sins in the light of thy countenance.
For all our days are passed away in thy wrath:
We spend our years as a tale that is told.
The days of our years are threescore years and ten:
And if by reason of strength they be fourscore years,
Yet is their strength labor and sorrow;

For it is soon cut off, and we fly away.
Who knoweth the power of thine anger?
Even according to thy fear, so is thy wrath.
So teach us to number our days,
That we may apply our hearts unto wisdom.
Return, O LORD, how long?
And let it repent thee concerning thy servants.
O satisfy us early with thy mercy;
That we may rejoice and be glad all our days.
Make us glad according to the days wherein thou hast afflicted us,
And the years wherein we have seen evil.
Let thy work appear unto thy servants,
And thy glory unto their children.
And let the beauty of the LORD our God be upon us:
And establish thou the work of our hands upon us; yea, the work of our hands establish thou it.

SIXTEENTH DAY OF THE MONTH.

Afternoon.

PSALM XCI.

HE that dwelleth in the secret place of the Most High
Shall abide under the shadow of the Almighty.
I will say of the LORD, He is my refuge and my fortress:
My God; in him will I trust.

Surely he shall deliver thee from the snare of the fowler,
And from the noisome pestilence.
He shall cover thee with his feathers, and under his wings shalt thou trust:
His truth shall be thy shield and buckler.
Thou shalt not be afraid for the terror by night;
Nor for the arrow that flieth by day;
Nor for the pestilence that walketh in darkness;
Nor for the destruction that wasteth at noonday.
A thousand shall fall at thy side, and ten thousand at thy right hand;
But it shall not come nigh thee.
Only with thine eyes shalt thou behold
And see the reward of the wicked.
Because thou hast made the Lord which is my refuge,
Even the Most High, thy habitation;
There shall no evil befall thee,
Neither shall any plague come nigh thy dwelling.
For he shall give his angels charge over thee,
To keep thee in all thy ways.
They shall bear thee up in their hands,
Lest thou dash thy foot against a stone.
Thou shalt tread upon the lion and adder:
The young lion and the dragon shalt thou trample under feet.
Because he hath set his love upon me, therefore will I deliver him:

I will set him on high, because he hath known my name.

He shall call upon me, and I will answer him: I will be with him in trouble;

I will deliver him, and honor him.

With long life will I satisfy him,

And show him my salvation.

SEVENTEENTH DAY OF THE MONTH.

𝔐orning.

Psalm XCIV.

THE Lord knoweth the thoughts of man,
That they are vanity.
Blessed is the man whom thou chastenest, O Lord,
And teachest him out of thy law;
For the Lord will not cast off his people,
Neither will he forsake his inheritance.
But judgment shall return unto righteousness:
And all the upright in heart shall follow it.
Unless the Lord had been my help,
My soul had almost dwelt in silence.
When I said, My foot slippeth;
Thy mercy, O Lord, held me up.
In the multitude of my thoughts within me
Thy comforts delight my soul.
The Lord is my defence;
And my God is the rock of my refuge.

Psalm XCV.

O COME, let us sing unto the LORD:
Let us make a joyful noise to the Rock of our salvation.
Let us come before his presence with thanksgiving,
And make a joyful noise unto him with psalms.
For the LORD is a great God,
And a great King above all gods.
In his hand are the deep places of the earth:
The strength of the hills is his also.
The sea is his, and he made it:
And his hands formed the dry land.
O come, let us worship and bow down:
Let us kneel before the Lord our maker.
For he is our God;
And we are the people of his pasture, and the sheep of his hand.
To-day if ye will hear his voice, harden not your heart, as in the provocation,
And as in the day of temptation in the wilderness:
When your fathers tempted me,
Proved me, and saw my work.
Forty years long was I grieved with this generation, and said, It is a people that do err in their heart,
And they have not known my ways:
Unto whom I sware in my wrath,
That they should not enter into my rest.

SEVENTEENTH DAY OF THE MONTH.

Afternoon.

Psalm XCVI.

O SING unto the Lord a new song:
Sing unto the Lord, all the earth,
Sing unto the Lord, bless his name;
Show forth his salvation from day to day.
Declare his glory among the heathen,
His wonders among all people.
For the Lord is great, and greatly to be praised:
He is to be feared above all gods.
For all the gods of the nations are idols:
But the Lord made the heavens.
Honor and majesty are before him:
Strength and beauty are in his sanctuary.
Give unto the Lord, O ye kindreds of the people,
Give unto the Lord glory and strength.
Give unto the Lord the glory due unto his name:
Bring an offering, and come into his courts.
O worship the Lord in the beauty of holiness;
Fear before him, all the earth.
Say among the heathen that the Lord reigneth: the world also shall be established that it shall not be moved:
He shall judge the people righteously.
Let the heavens rejoice, and let the earth be glad;
Let the sea roar, and the fulness thereof.

Let the field be joyful, and all that is therein;
Then shall all the trees of the wood rejoice.
Before the Lord; for he cometh,
For he cometh to judge the earth:
He shall judge the world with righteousness,
And the people with his truth.

Psalm XCVII.

THE Lord reigneth; let the earth rejoice;
  Let the multitude of isles be glad thereof.
Clouds and darkness are round about him:
Righteousness and judgment are the habitation of his throne.
The heavens declare his righteousness,
And all the people see his glory.
Zion heard, and was glad; and the daughters of Judah rejoiced,
Because of thy judgments, O Lord.
For thou, Lord, art high above all the earth:
Thou art exalted far above all gods.
Ye that love the Lord, hate evil: he preserveth the souls of his saints;
He delivereth them out of the hand of the wicked.
Light is sown for the righteous,
And gladness for the upright in heart.
Rejoice in the Lord, ye righteous,
And give thanks at the remembrance of his holiness.

EIGHTEENTH DAY OF THE MONTH.

Morning.

Psalm XCVIII.

O SING unto the Lord a new song; for he hath done marvellous things:

His right hand, and his holy arm, hath gotten him the victory.

The Lord hath made known his salvation:

His righteousness hath he openly showed in the sight of the heathen.

He hath remembered his mercy and his truth toward the house of Israel:

All the ends of the earth have seen the salvation of our God.

Make a joyful noise unto the Lord, all the earth:

Make a loud noise, and rejoice, and sing praise.

Sing unto the Lord with the harp;

With the harp, and the voice of a psalm.

With trumpets and sound of cornet

Make a joyful noise before the Lord, the King.

Let the sea roar, and the fulness thereof;

The world, and they that dwell therein.

Let the floods clap their hands:

Let the hills be joyful together,

Before the Lord; for he cometh to judge the earth;

With righteousness shall he judge the world, and the people with equity.

Psalm XCIII.

THE LORD reigneth,
He is clothed with majesty:
The LORD is clothed with strength, wherewith he hath girded himself.
The world also is established, that it cannot be moved.
Thy throne is established of old:
Thou art from everlasting.
The floods have lifted up, O LORD, the floods have lifted up their voice;
The floods lift up their waves.
The LORD on high is mightier than the noise of many waters,
Yea, than the mighty waves of the sea.
Thy testimonies are very sure:
Holiness becometh thine house, O Lord, for ever.

EIGHTEENTH DAY OF THE MONTH.

Afternoon.

Psalm XCIX.

THE LORD reigneth; let the people tremble:
He sitteth between the cherubim; let the earth be moved.
The LORD is great in Zion;
And he is high above all the people.

Let them praise thy great and terrible name;
For it is holy.
Exalt ye the LORD our God,
And worship at his footstool; for he is holy.
Moses and Aaron among his priests, and Samuel among them that call upon his name;
They called upon the Lord, and he answered them.
He spake unto them in the cloudy pillar:
They kept his testimonies, and the ordinance that he gave them.
Exalt the LORD our God, and worship at his holy hill;
For the Lord our God is holy.

PSALM C.

MAKE a joyful noise unto the LORD, all ye lands.
Serve the Lord with gladness: come before his presence with singing.
Know ye that the LORD he is God: it is he that hath made us, and not we ourselves;
We are his people, and the sheep of his pasture.
Enter into his gates with thanksgiving, and into his courts with praise:
Be thankful unto him, and bless his name.
For the LORD is good; his mercy is everlasting;
And his truth endureth to all generations.

NINETEENTH DAY OF THE MONTH.

𝔐orning.

Psalm CIII.

Bless the Lord, O my soul:
And all that is within me, bless his holy name.
Bless the Lord, O my soul,
And forget not all his benefits:
Who forgiveth all thine iniquities;
Who healeth all thy diseases;
Who redeemeth thy life from destruction;
Who crowneth thee with loving-kindness and tender mercies;
Who satisfieth thy mouth with good things;
So that thy youth is renewed like the eagle's.
The Lord executeth righteousness,
And judgment for all that are oppressed.
He made known his ways unto Moses,
His acts unto the children of Israel.
The Lord is merciful and gracious,
Slow to anger, and plenteous in mercy.
He will not always chide;
Neither will he keep his anger for ever.
He hath not dealt with us after our sins;
Nor rewarded us according to our iniquities.
For as the heaven is high above the earth,
So great is his mercy toward them that fear him.

As far as the east is from the west,
So far hath he removed our transgressions from us.
Like as a father pitieth his children,
So the Lord pitieth them that fear him.
For he knoweth our frame;
He remembereth that we are dust.
As for man, his days are as grass:
As a flower of the field, so he flourisheth.
For the wind passeth over it, and it is gone;
And the place thereof shall know it no more.
But the mercy of the LORD is from everlasting to everlasting upon them that fear him.
And his righteousness unto children's children;
To such as keep his covenant,
And to those that remember his commandments to do them.
The LORD hath prepared his throne in the heavens;
And his kingdom ruleth over all.
Bless the LORD, ye his angels, that excel in strength,
That do his commandments, hearkening unto the voice of his word.
Bless ye the LORD, all ye his hosts;
Ye ministers of his, that do his pleasure.
Bless the LORD, all his works, in all places of his dominion:
Bless the Lord, O my soul.

NINETEENTH DAY OF THE MONTH.

Afternoon.

Psalm CIV.

BLESS the LORD, O my soul. O LORD my God, thou art very great;
Thou art clothed with honor and majesty:
Who coverest thyself with light as with a garment:
Who stretchest out the heavens like a curtain:
Who layeth the beams of his chambers in the waters: who maketh the clouds his chariot:
Who walketh upon the wings of the wind:
Who maketh his angels spirits;
His ministers a flaming fire:
Who laid the foundations of the earth,
That it should not be removed for ever.
He appointed the moon for seasons:
The sun knoweth his going down.
Thou makest darkness, and it is night:
Wherein all the beasts of the forest do creep forth.
The young lions roar after their prey,
And seek their meat from God.
The sun ariseth, they gather themselves together,
And lay them down in their dens.
Man goeth forth unto his work
And to his labor until the evening.
O LORD, how manifold are thy works! in wisdom hast thou made them all:

The earth is full of thy riches.

So is this great and wide sea, wherein are things creeping innumerable,

Both small and great beasts.

There go the ships:

There is that leviathan, whom thou hast made to play therein.

These wait all upon thee;

That thou mayest give them their meat in due season.

That thou givest them, they gather:

Thou openest thine hand, they are filled with good.

Thou hidest thy face, they are troubled:

Thou takest away their breath, they die, and return to their dust.

Thou sendest forth thy spirit, they are created:

And thou renewest the face of the earth.

The glory of the LORD shall endure for ever:

The Lord shall rejoice in his works.

He looketh on the earth, and it trembleth:

He toucheth the hills, and they smoke.

I will sing unto the LORD as long as I live:

I will sing praise to my God while I have my being.

My meditation of him shall be sweet:

I will be glad in the Lord.

Bless thou the LORD, O my soul.

Praise ye the Lord.

TWENTIETH DAY OF THE MONTH.

Morning.

Psalm CV.

O GIVE thanks unto the Lord; call upon his name:
Make known his deeds among the people.
Sing unto him, sing psalms unto him:
Talk ye of all his wondrous works.
Glory ye in his holy name:
Let the heart of them rejoice that seek the Lord.
Seek the Lord, and his strength:
Seek his face evermore.
Remember his marvellous works that he hath done;
His wonders, and the judgments of his mouth;
O ye seed of Abraham his servant,
Ye children of Jacob his chosen.
He is the Lord our God:
His judgments are in all the earth.
He hath remembered his covenant for ever,
The word which he commanded to a thousand generations.

Psalm CVI.

PRAISE ye the Lord. O give thanks unto the Lord;
For he is good: for his mercy endureth for ever.
Who can utter the mighty acts of the Lord?
Who can show forth all his praise?
Blessed are they that keep judgment,
And he that doeth righteousness at all times.
Remember me, O Lord, with the favor that thou bearest unto thy people:
O visit me with thy salvation;
That I may see the good of thy chosen, that I may rejoice in the gladness of thy nation,
That I may glory with thine inheritance.
We have sinned with our fathers, we have committed iniquity,
We have done wickedly.
Save us, O Lord our God, and gather us from among the heathen,
To give thanks unto thy holy name, and to triumph in thy praise.
Blessed be the Lord God of Israel from everlasting to everlasting:
And let all the people say, Amen.

TWENTIETH DAY OF THE MONTH.

Afternoon.

Psalm CVII.

O GIVE thanks unto the Lord, for he is good:
For his mercy endureth for ever.
Let the redeemed of the Lord say so,
Whom he hath redeemed from the hand of the enemy:
And gathered them out of the lands,
From the east, and from the west, from the north, and from the south.
They wandered in the wilderness in a solitary way;
They found no city to dwell in.
Hungry and thirsty,
Their soul fainted in them.
Then they cried unto the Lord in their trouble,
And he delivered them out of their distresses.
And he led them forth by the right way,
That they might go to a city of habitation.
Oh that men would praise the Lord for his goodness,
And for his wonderful works to the children of men!
For he satisfieth the longing soul,
And filleth the hungry soul with goodness.

Such as sit in darkness and the shadow of death,
Being bound in affliction and iron;
Because they rebelled against the words of God,
And contemned the counsel of the Most High:
Therefore he brought down their heart with labor;
They fell down, and there was none to help.
Then they cried unto the LORD in their trouble,
And he saved them out of their distresses.
He brought them out of darkness and the shadow of death,
And brake their bands in sunder.
Oh that men would praise the LORD for his goodness,
And for his wonderful works to the children of men!
For he hath broken the gates of brass,
And cut the bars of iron in sunder.
Fools, because of their transgression,
And because of their iniquities, are afflicted.
Their soul abhorreth all manner of meat;
And they draw near unto the gates of death.
Then they cry unto the LORD in their trouble,
And he saveth them out of their distresses.
He sent his word, and healed them,
And delivered them from their destructions.

TWENTY-FIRST DAY OF THE MONTH.

Morning.

Psalm CVII.

OH that men would praise the Lord for his goodness,
And for his wonderful works to the children of men!
And let them sacrifice the sacrifices of thanksgiving,
And declare his works with rejoicing.
They that go down to the sea in ships,
That do business in great waters;
These see the works of the Lord,
And his wonders in the deep.
For he commandeth, and raiseth the stormy wind,
Which lifteth up the waves thereof.
They mount up to the heaven, they go down again to the depths:
Their soul is melted because of trouble.
They reel to and fro, and stagger like a drunken man,
And are at their wit's end.
Then they cry unto the Lord in their trouble,
And he bringeth them out of their distresses.
He maketh the storm a calm,
So that the waves thereof are still.
Then are they glad because they be quiet;
So he bringeth them unto their desired haven.
Oh that men would praise the Lord for his goodness,

And for his wonderful works to the children of men!
Let them exalt him also in the congregation of the people,
And praise him in the assembly of the elders.
He turneth rivers into a wilderness,
And the watersprings into dry ground;
A fruitful land into barrenness,
For the wickedness of them that dwell therein.
He turneth the wilderness into a standing water,
And dry ground into watersprings.
And there he maketh the hungry to dwell,
That they may prepare a city for habitation;
And sow the fields, and plant vineyards,
Which may yield fruits of increase.
He blesseth them also, so that they are multiplied greatly:
And suffereth not their cattle to decrease.
Again, they are minished and brought low
Through oppression, affliction, and sorrow.
He poureth contempt upon princes,
And causeth them to wander in the wilderness, where there is no way.
Yet setteth he the poor on high from affliction,
And maketh him families like a flock.
The righteous shall see it, and rejoice:
And all iniquity shall stop her mouth.
Whoso is wise, and will observe these things,
Even they shall understand the loving-kindness of the Lord.

TWENTY-FIRST DAY OF THE MONTH.

Afternoon.

Psalm CXI.

PRAISE ye the Lord. I will praise the Lord with my whole heart,
In the assembly of the upright and in the congregation.
The works of the Lord are great,
Sought out of all them that have pleasure therein.
His work is honorable and glorious:
And his righteousness endureth for ever.
He hath made his wonderful works to be remembered:
The Lord is gracious and full of compassion.
He hath given meat unto them that fear him:
He will ever be mindful of his covenant.
He hath showed his people the power of his works,
That he may give them the heritage of the heathen.
The works of his hands are verity and judgment;
All his commandments are sure.
They stand fast for ever and ever,
And are done in truth and uprightness.
He sent redemption unto his people: he hath commanded his covenant for ever:
Holy and reverend is his name.
The fear of the Lord is the beginning of wisdom:
A good understanding have all they that do his commandments: his praise endureth for ever.

Psalm CXII.

PRAISE ye the Lord. Blessed is the man that feareth the Lord,
That delighteth greatly in his commandments.
Unto the upright there ariseth light in the darkness.
He is gracious, and full of compassion, and righteous.
A good man showeth favor, and lendeth:
He will guide his affairs with discretion.
Surely he shall not be moved for ever:
The righteous shall be in everlasting remembrance.
He shall not be afraid of evil tidings:
His heart is fixed, trusting in the Lord.
He hath dispersed, he hath given to the poor; his righteousness endureth for ever;
His horn shall be exalted with honor.

TWENTY-SECOND DAY OF THE MONTH.
Morning.
Psalm CXIII.

PRAISE ye the Lord. Praise, O ye servants of the Lord,
Praise the name of the Lord.
Blessed be the name of the Lord
From this time forth and for evermore.
From the rising of the sun unto the going down of the same
The Lord's name is to be praised.

The Lord is high above all nations,
And his glory above the heavens.
Who is like unto the Lord our God,
Who dwelleth on high,
Who humbleth himself to behold
The things that are in heaven, and in the earth?

Psalm CXV.

NOT unto us, O Lord, not unto us, but unto thy name give glory,
For thy mercy, and for thy truth's sake.
Wherefore should the heathen say,
Where is now their God?
But our God is in the heavens:
He hath done whatsoever he hath pleased.
Their idols are silver and gold,
The work of men's hands.
The Lord shall increase you more and more,
You and your children.
Ye are blessed of the Lord
Which made heaven and earth.
The heaven, even the heavens, are the Lord's:
But the earth hath he given to the children of men.
The dead praise not the Lord,
Neither any that go down into silence.
But we will bless the Lord
From this time forth and for evermore. Praise the Lord.

TWENTY-SECOND DAY OF THE MONTH.

Afternoon.

Psalm CXVI.

I LOVE the LORD, because he hath heard my voice
And my supplications.
Because he hath inclined his ear unto me,
Therefore will I call upon him as long as I live.
Gracious is the LORD, and righteous,
Yea, our God is merciful.
The LORD preserveth the simple.
I was brought low, and he helped me.
Return unto thy rest, O my soul;
For the Lord hath dealt bountifully with thee.
For thou hast delivered my soul from death,
Mine eyes from tears, and my feet from falling.
I will walk before the LORD
In the land of the living.
What shall I render unto the LORD for all his benefits toward me?
I will take the cup of salvation, and call upon the name of the Lord.
I will pay my vows unto the LORD now
In the presence of all his people.
O LORD, truly I am thy servant;
I am thy servant, and the son of thine handmaid:
I will offer to thee the sacrifice of thanksgiving,
And will call upon the name of the Lord.

I will pay my vows unto the LORD now in the presence of all his people,

In the courts of the Lord's house, in the midst of thee, O Jerusalem.

TWENTY-THIRD DAY OF THE MONTH.

Morning.

Psalm CXVIII.

O GIVE thanks unto the LORD; for he is good:
Because his mercy endureth for ever.
Let them now that fear the LORD say,
That his mercy endureth for ever.
I called upon the LORD in distress:
The Lord answered me, and set me in a large place.
It is better to trust in the LORD
Than to put confidence in man.
It is better to trust in the LORD
Than to put confidence in princes.
The LORD is my strength and song,
And is become my salvation.
The voice of rejoicing and salvation is in the tabernacles of the righteous:
The right hand of the Lord doeth valiantly.
The right hand of the LORD is exalted:
The right hand of the Lord doeth valiantly.

I shall not die, but live,
And declare the works of the Lord.
The LORD hath chastened me sore:
But he hath not given me over unto death.
Open to me the gates of righteousness:
I will go into them, and I will praise the Lord:
This gate of the LORD,
Into which the righteous shall enter.
I will praise thee: for thou hast heard me,
And art become my salvation.
The stone which the builders refused
Is become the head stone of the corner.
This is the LORD's doing;
It is marvellous in our eyes.
This is the day which the LORD hath made;
We will rejoice and be glad in it.
Save now, I beseech thee, O LORD:
O Lord, I beseech thee, send now prosperity.
Blessed be he that cometh in the name of the LORD;
We have blessed you out of the house of the Lord.
God is the LORD, which hath showed us light:
Thou art my God, and I will praise thee:
O give thanks unto the LORD; for he is good:
For his mercy endureth for ever.

TWENTY-THIRD DAY OF THE MONTH.

Afternoon.

Psalm CXIX.

O HOW love I thy law!
It is my meditation all the day.
Thou through thy commandments hast made me wiser than mine enemies:
For they are ever with me.
I have more understanding than all my teachers:
For thy testimonies are my meditation.
I understand more than the ancients,
Because I keep thy precepts.
I have refrained my feet from every evil way,
That I might keep thy word.
I have not departed from thy judgments:
For thou hast taught me.
How sweet are thy words unto my taste!
Yea, sweeter than honey to my mouth.
Through thy precepts I get understanding:
Therefore I hate every false way.
Thy word is a lamp unto my feet,
And a light unto my path.
I have sworn, and I will perform it,
That I will keep thy righteous judgments.
I am afflicted very much:
Quicken me, O Lord, according unto thy word.

Accept, I beseech thee, the freewill offerings of my mouth, O LORD,
And teach me thy judgments.
My soul is continually in my hand:
Yet do I not forget thy law.
The wicked have laid a snare for me:
Yet I erred not from thy precepts.
Thy testimonies have I taken as an heritage for ever:
For they are the rejoicing of my heart.
I have inclined mine heart to perform thy statutes
Always, even unto the end.
I hate vain thoughts:
But thy law do I love.
Thou art my hiding place and my shield:
I hope in thy word.

TWENTY-FOURTH DAY OF THE MONTH.

Morning.

PSALM CXIX.

GREAT are thy tender mercies, O LORD:
Quicken me according to thy judgments.
Many are my persecutors and mine enemies:
Yet do I not decline from thy testimonies.
I beheld the transgressors, and was grieved;
Because they kept not thy word.

Consider how I love thy precepts:
Quicken me, O Lord, according to thy loving-kindness.

Thy word is true from the beginning:
And every one of thy righteous judgments endureth for ever.

Depart from me, ye evil doers:
For I will keep the commandments of my God.

Uphold me according unto thy word, that I may live:
And let me not be ashamed of my hope.

Hold thou me up, and I shall be safe:
And I will have respect unto thy statutes continually.

Thou hast trodden down all them that err from thy statutes:
For their deceit is falsehood.

Thou puttest away all the wicked of the earth like dross:
Therefore I love thy testimonies.

My flesh trembleth for fear of thee;
And I am afraid of thy judgments.

I have done judgment and justice:
Leave me not to mine oppressors.

Be surety for thy servant for good:
Let not the proud oppress me.

Mine eyes fail for thy salvation,
And for the word of thy righteousness.

Deal with thy servant according unto thy mercy,
And teach me thy statutes.

I am thy servant; give me understanding,
That I may know thy testimonies.
It is time for thee, LORD, to work:
For they have made void thy law.
Therefore I love thy commandments
Above gold; yea, above fine gold.
Therefore I esteem all thy precepts concerning all things to be right;
And I hate every false way.

TWENTY-FOURTH DAY OF THE MONTH.
Afternoon.

PSALM CXIX.

THY testimonies are wonderful:
Therefore doth my soul keep them.
The entrance of thy words giveth light;
It giveth understanding unto the simple.
Look thou upon me, and be merciful unto me,
As thou usest to do unto those that love thy name.
Order my steps in thy word:
And let not any iniquity have dominion over me.
Deliver me from the oppression of man;
So will I keep thy precepts.
Make thy face to shine upon thy servant:
And teach me thy statutes.

Righteous art thou, O Lord,
And upright are thy judgments.
Thy testimonies that thou hast commanded are righteous
And very faithful.
Thy word is very pure:
Therefore thy servant loveth it.
I am small and despised;
Yet do not I forget thy precepts.
Thy righteousness is an everlasting righteousness,
And thy law is the truth.
Trouble and anguish have taken hold on me:
Yet thy commandments are my delights.
The righteousness of thy testimonies is everlasting:
Give me understanding, and I shall live.
I cried with my whole heart; hear me, O Lord:
I will keep thy statutes.
I cried unto thee: save me,
And I shall keep thy testimonies.
Hear my voice, according unto thy loving-kindness:
O Lord, quicken me according to thy judgment.
They draw nigh that follow after mischief,
They are far from thy law.
Thou art near, O Lord;
And all thy commandments are truth.

TWENTY-FIFTH DAY OF THE MONTH.

𝔐orning.

Psalm CXXI.

I WILL lift up mine eyes unto the hills,
From whence cometh my help.
My help cometh from the Lord
Which made heaven and earth.
He will not suffer thy foot to be moved:
He that keepeth thee will not slumber.
Behold, he that keepeth Israel
Shall neither slumber nor sleep.
The Lord is thy keeper:
The Lord is thy shade upon thy right hand.
The sun shall not smite thee by day,
Nor the moon by night.
The Lord shall preserve thee from all evil:
He shall preserve thy soul.
The Lord shall preserve thy going out and thy coming in
From this time forth, and even for evermore.

Psalm CXXII.

I WAS glad when they said unto me,
Let us go into the house of the Lord.
Our feet shall stand within thy gates, O Jerusalem.

Jerusalem is builded as a city that is compact together:

Whither the tribes go up, the tribes of the LORD,

Unto the testimony of Israel, to give thanks unto the name of the Lord.

For there are set thrones of judgment,

The thrones of the house of David.

Pray for the peace of Jerusalem:

They shall prosper that love thee.

Peace be within thy walls,

And prosperity within thy palaces.

For my brethren and companions' sakes,

I will now say, Peace be within thee.

Because of the house of the LORD our God,

I will seek thy good.

TWENTY-FIFTH DAY OF THE MONTH.

Afternoon.

PSALM CXXIII.

UNTO thee lift I up mine eyes,

O thou that dwellest in the heavens.

Behold, as the eyes of servants look unto the hand of their masters,

And as the eyes of a maiden unto the hand of her mistress;

So our eyes wait upon the LORD our God,
Until that he have mercy upon us.

Have mercy upon us, O LORD, have mercy upon us:
For we are exceedingly filled with contempt.

Our soul is exceedingly filled with the scorning of those that are at ease,
And with the contempt of the proud.

Psalm CXXV.

THEY that trust in the LORD shall be as Mount Zion,
Which cannot be removed, but abideth for ever.

As the mountains are round about Jerusalem,
So the Lord is round about his people, from henceforth even for ever.

For the rod of the wicked shall not rest upon the lot of the righteous;
Lest the righteous put forth their hands unto iniquity.

Do good, O LORD, unto those that be good,
And to them that are upright in their hearts.

TWENTY-SIXTH DAY OF THE MONTH.

Morning.

Psalm CXXXVIII.

I WILL praise thee with my whole heart:
Before the gods will I sing praise unto thee.
I will worship toward thy holy temple,
And praise thy name
For thy loving-kindness and for thy truth:
For thou hast magnified thy word above all thy name.
In the day when I cried thou answeredst me,
And strengthenedst me with strength in my soul.
All the kings of the earth shall praise thee, O Lord,
When they hear the words of thy mouth.
Yea, they shall sing in the ways of the Lord:
For great is the glory of the Lord.
Though the Lord be high, yet hath he respect unto the lowly:
But the proud he knoweth afar off.
Though I walk in the midst of trouble, thou wilt revive me:
Thou shalt stretch forth thine hand against the wrath of mine enemies, and thy right hand shall save me.
The Lord will perfect that which concerneth me: thy mercy, O Lord, endureth for ever:
Forsake not the works of thine own hands.

TWENTY-SIXTH DAY OF THE MONTH.
Afternoon.
Psalm CXXXIX.

O LORD, thou hast searched me, and known me.
Thou knowest my down-sitting and my up-rising,
Thou understandest my thought afar off.
Thou compassest my path and my lying down,
And art acquainted with all my ways.
For there is not a word in my tongue,
But lo, O Lord, thou knowest it altogether.
Thou hast beset me behind and before,
And laid thine hand upon me.
Such knowledge is too wonderful for me;
It is high, I cannot attain unto it.
Whither shall I go from thy spirit?
Or whither shall I flee from thy presence?
If I ascend up into heaven, thou art there:
If I make my bed in hell, behold thou art there.
If I take the wings of the morning,
And dwell in the uttermost parts of the sea;
Even there shall thy hand lead me,
And thy right hand shall hold me.
If I say, Surely the darkness shall cover me;
Even the night shall be light about me.
Yea, the darkness hideth not from thee; but the night shineth as the day:
The darkness and the light are both alike to thee.

I will praise thee; for I am fearfully and wonderfully made:
Marvellous are thy works; and that my soul knoweth right well.
How precious also are thy thoughts unto me, O God!
How great is the sum of them!
If I should count them, they are more in number than the sand:
When I awake, I am still with thee.
Search me, O God, and know my heart:
Try me, and know my thoughts:
And see if there be any wicked way in me,
And lead me in the way everlasting.

TWENTY-SEVENTH DAY OF THE MONTH.
Morning.

Psalm CXLV.

I WILL extol thee, my God, O King,
And I will bless thy name for ever and ever.
Every day will I bless thee;
And I will praise thy name for ever and ever.
Great is the Lord, and greatly to be praised;
And his greatness is unsearchable.
One generation shall praise thy works to another,
And shall declare thy mighty acts.

I will speak of the glorious honor of thy majesty,
And of thy wondrous works.

And men shall speak of the might of thy terrible acts:
And I will declare thy greatness.

They shall abundantly utter the memory of thy great goodness,
And shall sing of thy righteousness.

The LORD is gracious and full of compassion;
Slow to anger, and of great mercy.

The LORD is good to all:
And his tender mercies are over all his works.

All thy works shall praise thee, O LORD;
And thy saints shall bless thee.

They shall speak of the glory of thy kingdom,
And talk of thy power;

To make known to the sons of men his mighty acts,
And the glorious majesty of his kingdom.

Thy kingdom is an everlasting kingdom,
And thy dominion endureth throughout all generations.

The LORD upholdeth all that fall,
And raiseth up all those that be bowed down.

The eyes of all wait upon thee:
And thou givest them their meat in due season.

Thou openest thine hand,
And satisfiest the desire of every living thing.

The LORD is righteous in all his ways,
And holy in all his works.

The LORD is nigh unto all them that call upon him,
To all that call upon him in truth.
He will fulfill the desire of them that fear him:
He also will hear their cry, and will save them.
The LORD preserveth all them that love him:
But all the wicked will he destroy.
My mouth shall speak the praise of the LORD:
And let all flesh bless his holy name for ever and ever.

TWENTY-SEVENTH DAY OF THE MONTH.
Afternoon.

PSALM CXLVI.

PRAISE ye the LORD.
Praise the Lord, O my soul.
While I live will I praise the LORD:
I will sing praises unto my God while I have any being.
Put not your trust in princes,
Nor in the son of man, in whom there is no help.
His breath goeth forth, he returneth to his earth;
In that very day his thoughts perish.
Happy is he that hath the God of Jacob for his help,
Whose hope is in the Lord his God:

Which made heaven, and earth, the sea, and all that therein is:

Which keepeth truth for ever:

Which executeth judgment for the oppressed:

Which giveth food to the hungry.

The Lord looseth the prisoners:

The Lord openeth the eyes of the blind:

The Lord raiseth them that are bowed down:

The Lord loveth the righteous:

The Lord preserveth the strangers: he relieveth the fatherless and widow;

But the way of the wicked he turneth upside down.

The Lord shall reign for ever,

Even thy God, O Zion, unto all generations. Praise ye the Lord.

TWENTY-EIGHTH DAY OF THE MONTH.

Morning.

Psalm CXLVII.

PRAISE ye the Lord: for it is good to sing praises unto our God;

For it is pleasant; and praise is comely.

The Lord doth build up Jerusalem:

He gathereth together the outcasts of Israel.

He healeth the broken in heart,

And bindeth up their wounds.

He telleth the number of the stars;
He calleth them all by their names.
Great is our Lord, and of great power:
His understanding is infinite.
The Lord lifteth up the meek:
He casteth the wicked down to the ground.
Sing unto the Lord with thanksgiving;
Sing praise upon the harp unto our God:
Who covereth the heaven with clouds, who prepareth rain for the earth,
Who maketh grass to grow upon the mountains.
He giveth to the beast his food,
And to the young ravens which cry.
He delighteth not in the strength of the horse:
He taketh not pleasure in the legs of a man.
The Lord taketh pleasure in them that fear him,
In those that hope in his mercy.
Praise the Lord, O Jerusalem;
Praise thy God, O Zion.
For he hath strengthened the bars of thy gates,
He hath blessed thy children within thee.
He maketh peace in thy borders,
And filleth thee with the finest of the wheat.
He sendeth forth his commandment upon earth:
His word runneth very swiftly.
He giveth snow like wool:
He scattereth the hoar frost like ashes.
He casteth forth his ice like morsels:
Who can stand before his cold?

He sendeth out his word, and melteth them:
He causeth his wind to blow, and the waters flow.
He showeth his word unto Jacob,
His statutes and his judgments unto Israel.
He hath not dealt so with any nation:
And as for his judgments, they have not known them.
Praise ye the Lord.

TWENTY-EIGHTH DAY OF THE MONTH.
Afternoon.
Psalm CXLVIII.

PRAISE ye the Lord. Praise ye the Lord from the heavens:
Praise him in the heights.
Praise ye him, all his angels:
Praise ye him, all his hosts.
Praise ye him, sun and moon:
Praise him, all ye stars of light.
Praise him, ye heavens of heavens,
And ye waters that be above the heavens.
Let them praise the name of the Lord:
For he commanded, and they were created.
He hath also established them for ever and ever:
He hath made a decree which shall not pass.
Praise the Lord from the earth,
Ye dragons, and all deeps:

Fire, and hail; snow, and vapor:
Stormy wind fulfilling his word:
Mountains, and all hills;
Fruitful trees, and all cedars:
Beasts, and all cattle;
Creeping things, and flying fowl:
Kings of the earth, and all people;
Princes, and all judges of the earth:
Both young men, and maidens;
Old men, and children:
Let them praise the name of the LORD: for his name alone is excellent;
His glory is above the earth and heaven.
He also exalteth the horn of his people,
The praise of all his saints;
Even of the children of Israel, a people near unto him.
Praise ye the Lord.

PSALM CL.

PRAISE ye the LORD. Praise God in his sanctuary:
Praise him in the firmament of his power.
Praise him for his mighty acts:
Praise him according to his excellent greatness.
Praise him with the sound of the trumpet:

Praise him with the psaltery and harp.
Praise him with the timbrel and dance:
Praise him with stringed instruments and organs.
Praise him upon the loud cymbals:
Praise him upon the high sounding cymbals.
Let everything that hath breath praise the LORD.
Praise ye the Lord.

TWENTY-NINTH DAY OF THE MONTH.

𝔐orning.

ISAIAH XI.

AND there shall come forth a rod out of the stem of Jesse,
And a branch shall grow out of his roots:
And the spirit of the LORD shall rest upon him,
The spirit of wisdom and understanding,
The spirit of counsel and might,
The spirit of knowledge and of the fear of the Lord;
And shall make him of quick understanding
In the fear of the Lord;
And he shall not judge after the sight of his eyes,
Neither reprove after the hearing of his ears:
But with righteousness shall he judge the poor,
And reprove with equity for the meek of the earth.

And he shall smite the earth with the rod of his mouth,
And with the breath of his lips shall he slay the wicked.
And righteousness shall be the girdle of his loins,
And faithfulness the girdle of his reins.
The wolf also shall dwell with the lamb,
And the leopard shall lie down with the kid;
And the calf and the young lion and the fatling together;
And a little child shall lead them.
And the cow and the bear shall feed; their young ones shall lie down together:
And the lion shall eat straw like the ox.
And the sucking child shall play on the hole of the asp,
And the weaned child shall put his hand on the cockatrice's den.
They shall not hurt nor destroy in all my holy mountain,
For the earth shall be full of the knowledge of the Lord, as the waters cover the sea.

TWENTY-NINTH DAY OF THE MONTH.
Afternoon.
Isaiah XL.

COMFORT ye, comfort ye my people, saith your God.
Speak ye comfortably to Jerusalem, and cry unto her,
That her warfare is accomplished, that her iniquity is pardoned:
For she hath received of the Lord's hand double for all her sins.
The voice of him that crieth in the wilderness, Prepare ye the way of the LORD,
Make straight in the desert a highway for our God.
Every valley shall be exalted,
And every mountain and hill shall be made low:
And the crooked shall be made straight,
And the rough places plain:
And the glory of the LORD shall be revealed, and all flesh shall see it together:
For the mouth of the Lord hath spoken it.
The voice said, Cry.
And he said, What shall I cry?
All flesh is grass,
And all the goodliness thereof is as the flower of the field:
The grass withereth, the flower fadeth: because the spirit of the LORD bloweth upon it:
Surely the people is grass.

The grass withereth, the flower fadeth:
But the word of our God shall stand for ever.
O Zion, that bringest good tidings, get thee up into the high mountain:
O Jerusalem, that bringest good tidings, lift up thy voice with strength;
Lift it up, be not afraid;
Say unto the cities of Judah, Behold your God!
Behold the Lord GOD will come with strong hand,
And his arm shall rule for him:
Behold, his reward is with him,
And his work before him.
He shall feed his flock like a shepherd:
He shall gather the lambs with his arm,
And carry them in his bosom,
And shall gently lead those that are with young.

THIRTIETH DAY OF THE MONTH.

Morning.

ISAIAH XLII.

BEHOLD my servant, whom I uphold;
Mine elect, in whom my soul delighteth;
I have put my spirit upon him:
He shall bring forth judgment to the Gentiles.
He shall not cry, nor lift up,
Nor cause his voice to be heard in the street.

A bruised reed shall he not break, and the smoking flax shall he not quench :
He shall bring forth judgment unto truth.
He shall not fail nor be discouraged, till he have set judgment in the earth :
And the isles shall wait for his law.
Thus saith God the LORD,
He that created the heavens, and stretched them out;
He that spread forth the earth,
And that which cometh out of it;
He that giveth breath unto the people upon it,
And spirit to them that walk therein :
I the LORD have called thee in righteousness,
And will hold thine hand, and will keep thee,
And give thee for a covenant of the people,
For a light of the Gentiles;
To open the blind eyes, to bring out the prisoners from the prison,
And them that sit in darkness out of the prison house.
I am the LORD: that is my name: and my glory will I not give to another,
Neither my praise to graven images.
Behold, the former things are come to pass, and new things do I declare :
Before they spring forth I tell you of them.
Sing unto the LORD a new song,
And his praise from the end of the earth,
Ye that go down to the sea, and all that is therein ;
The isles, and the inhabitants thereof.

THIRTIETH DAY OF THE MONTH.
Afternoon.
Isaiah LV.

HO, every one that thirsteth, come ye to the waters,
And he that hath no money; come ye, buy, and eat;
Yea, come, buy wine and milk
Without money and without price.
Wherefore do ye spend money for that which is not bread?
And your labor for that which satisfieth not?
Hearken diligently unto me, and eat ye that which is good,
And let your soul delight itself in fatness.
Incline your ear, and come unto me:
Hear, and your soul shall live;
And I will make an everlasting covenant with you,
Even the sure mercies of David.
Behold, I have given him for a witness to the people,
A leader and commander to the people.
Behold, thou shalt call a nation that thou knowest not,
And nations that knew not thee shall run unto thee,
Because of the Lord thy God, and for the Holy One of Israel;
For he hath glorified thee.

Seek ye the Lord while he may be found,
Call ye upon him while he is near:
Let the wicked forsake his way,
And the unrighteous man his thoughts:
And let him return unto the Lord, and he will have mercy upon him;
And to our God, for he will abundantly pardon.
For my thoughts are not your thoughts,
Neither are your ways my ways, saith the Lord.
For as the heavens are higher than the earth, so are my ways higher than your ways,
And my thoughts than your thoughts.
For as the rain cometh down, and the snow from heaven,
And returneth not thither,
But watereth the earth, and maketh it bring forth and bud,
That it may give seed to the sower, and bread to the eater:
So shall my word be that goeth forth out of my mouth:
It shall not return unto me void,
But it shall accomplish that which I please,
And it shall prosper in the thing whereto I sent it.
For ye shall go out with joy,
And be led forth with peace:
The mountains and the hills shall break forth before you into singing,
And all the trees of the field shall clap their hands.

Instead of the thorn shall come up the fir tree,
And instead of the brier shall come up the myrtle tree:
And it shall be to the Lord for a name,
For an everlasting sign that shall not be cut off.

THIRTY-FIRST DAY OF THE MONTH.

Morning.

Isaiah LX.

ARISE, shine; for thy light is come,
And the glory of the Lord is risen upon thee.
For behold, the darkness shall cover the earth,
And gross darkness the people:
But the Lord shall arise upon thee,
And his glory shall be seen upon thee.
And the Gentiles shall come to thy light,
And kings to the brightness of thy rising.
Lift up thine eyes round about, and see: all they gather themselves together,
They come to thee:
Thy sons shall come from far,
And thy daughters shall be nursed at thy side.
Then thou shalt see, and flow together,
And thine heart shall fear, and be enlarged;

Because the abundance of the sea shall be converted unto thee,
The forces of the Gentiles shall come unto thee.
The multitude of camels shall cover thee, the dromedaries of Midian and Ephah;
All they from Sheba shall come:
They shall bring gold and incense;
And they shall show forth the praises of the Lord.
All the flocks of Kedar shall be gathered together unto thee,
The rams of Nebaioth shall minister unto thee:
They shall come up with acceptance on mine altar,
And I will glorify the house of my glory.
Who are these that fly as a cloud,
And as the doves to their windows?
Surely the isles shall wait for me, and the ships of Tarshish first,
To bring thy sons from far, their silver and their gold with them,
Unto the name of the LORD thy God,
And to the Holy One of Israel, because he hath glorified thee.
And the sons of strangers shall build up thy walls,
And their kings shall minister unto thee:
For in my wrath I smote thee,
But in my favor have I had mercy on thee.
Therefore thy gates shall be open continually;
They shall not be shut day nor night;

That men may bring unto thee the forces of the Gentiles,

And that their kings may be brought.

For the nation and kingdom that will not serve thee shall perish:

Yea, those nations shall be utterly wasted.

THIRTY-FIRST DAY OF THE MONTH.

𝔄fternoon.

Isaiah LX.

THE glory of Lebanon shall come unto thee,
The fir tree, the pine tree, and the box together,
To beautify the place of my sanctuary;
And I will make the place of my feet glorious.
The sons also of them that afflicted thee shall come bending unto thee;
And all they that despised thee shall bow themselves down at the soles of thy feet;
And they shall call thee, The city of the Lord,
The Zion of the Holy One of Israel.
Whereas thou hast been forsaken and hated,
So that no man went through thee,
I will make thee an eternal excellency,
A joy of many generations.

And thou shalt know that I the Lord am thy Saviour
And thy Redeemer, the mighty One of Jacob.
For brass I will bring gold, and for iron I will bring silver,
And for wood brass, and for stones iron:
I will also make thy officers peace,
And thine exactors righteousness.
Violence shall no more be heard in thy land,
Wasting nor destruction within thy borders;
But thou shalt call thy walls Salvation,
And thy gates Praise.
The sun shall be no more thy light by day:
Neither for brightness shall the moon give light unto thee:
But the Lord shall be unto thee an everlasting light,
And thy God thy glory.
Thy sun shall no more go down;
Neither shall thy moon withdraw itself;
For the Lord shall be thine everlasting light,
And the days of thy mourning shall be ended.

Isaiah LXI.

THE Spirit of the Lord God is upon me;
Because the Lord hath anointed me to preach good tidings unto the meek;

He hath sent me to bind up the broken-hearted,
To proclaim liberty to the captives, and the opening of the prison to them that are bound.
To proclaim the acceptable year of the Lord, and the day of vengeance of our God;
To comfort all that mourn;
To appoint unto them that mourn in Zion,
To give unto them beauty for ashes,
The oil of joy for mourning,
The garment of praise for the spirit of heaviness;
That they might be called trees of righteousness,
The planting of the Lord, that he might be glorified.
And they shall build the old wastes,
They shall raise up the former desolations,
And they shall repair the waste cities,
The desolations of many generations.

www.ingramcontent.com/pod-product-compliance
Lightning Source LLC
Chambersburg PA
CBHW032104230426
43672CB00009B/1638